CONTINUING WORD PROCESSING

CAMILLA BRADLEY

JOHN MURRAY

© Camilla Bradley 1990

First published 1990
by John Murray (Publishers) Ltd
50 Albemarle Street
London W1X 4BD

Reprinted 1992, 1994

All rights reserved
Unauthorised duplication
contravenes applicable laws

Cover photograph:
ZEFA Picture Library

Printed in Great Britain by St Edmundsbury Press Ltd

British Library Cataloguing in Publication Data

Bradley, Camilla
 Continuing Word Processing
 1. Word processing
 I. Title
 652.5

ISBN 0-7195-4710-5

CONTENTS

Introduction and WP Operations Checklist   3

Unit 1 Search and Replace

1.1   Global search and replace   4
1.2   The search facility   7
1.3   Using prior information to replace text   11

Unit 2 Pagination

2.1   Page breaks   19
2.2   Beginnings and endings of pages   24
2.3   Setting a page length   29

Unit 3 Headers and Footers

3.1   Using headers   36
3.2   Using footers   40
3.3   Selective headers and footers   46

Unit 4 Dealing with Paragraphs

4.1   Inserting fresh information   51
4.2   Copying text within a document   55
4.3   Moving text in a multipage document   59

Unit 5 Inserting Stored Text

5.1   Storing phrases   66
5.2   Using stored phrases to create a document   68
5.3   Inserting stored text in a standard document   73

Unit 6 Tabs and Decimal Tabs

6.1   Setting text in columns   83
6.2   Decimal tabs   89
6.3   Widening the page   92

Unit 7 Style

7.1   Emboldening text   98
7.2   Pitch   101
7.3   Subscripts and superscripts   104
7.4   Special characters and hyphenation   107

Unit 8 Mail Merge

8.1   Merging names and addresses in standard letters   112
8.2   Merging other details   118
8.3   Selective merging   122

▶ Continued

Now key in the standard letter in Task 80, inserting merge codes at the points where variable information is to be merged. (These are marked here by an asterisk.) When you have completed it, proof read it carefully, store it on disc and print out a letter to everyone on the datafile who has a Pax computer.

TASK 80

Our ref MH/(your initials)

* (Today's date)

* (Name and address of addressee)

Dear * (Name)

NEW SOFTWARE

Our records show that you purchased a * (product) from our company. We should like to invite you to attend a demonstration of the new software that is now available for your machine.

We shall be holding demonstrations in the conference suite at the Cardiff International Hotel, and we enclose details of the dates and times available, together with a booking form.

We look forward to receiving your prompt reply.

Yours sincerely

MALCOLM HARDY
Promotions Manager

Enc

Unit 8: Selective merging

INTRODUCTION

Who the book is for

This book is for those of you who are familiar with the basic operation of a word processor and want to learn about its more advanced functions.

Some of you may have passed an elementary exam in word processing, but this is not necessary, so long as you can fulfil basic functions – such as centring and underlining text – without difficulty.

It is suitable for those of you following an intermediate or advanced word processing course, but as it is not necessary to have a tutor to guide you through the tasks, anyone who is an 'open learning' student or attending a word processing 'workshop' will find it useful too. The tasks are carefully graded to allow you to build up skill gradually, so it is possible to work through them on your own.

What it assumes

As you are not a beginner, it is assumed that you know the keyboard and can input text accurately at a reasonable speed. You must, of course, be able to start up your word processor and operate its elementary functions with ease.

You are also expected to have some knowledge of business practice, as many of the tasks consist of commercial correspondence, and you will have to be aware of customary usage when dealing with this. For example, you will have to know the acceptable styles for setting out a letter, and you will be expected to date it and mark any enclosures.

Some knowledge of exam theory is also assumed, and you will be expected to perform basic amendments to text which are indicated by standard correction signs.

Exam preparation

The book covers the word processing functions required for intermediate and advanced word processing exams and gives suitable preparation for the external exams of the RSA, LCCI and PEI. However, as the tasks pursue a broad commercial theme, the book can be used equally well by students following a more integrated business course, such as BTEC National or NVQ Level II or III.

How to proceed

As this book can be used with any hardware or software, you are advised to use the Checklist below to key in and print out your own notes on the word processing functions. These are specified in each unit before the tasks to which they relate. This means that you should make your notes before you attempt to key in the tasks. You should keep your Checklists for reference purposes and to help you revise for exam or assignment work.

WP OPERATIONS CHECKLIST

FUNCTION	HOW TO DO IT

TASK 80

This is a timed task which should take you no longer than 40 minutes to complete and print out.

Prepare this datafile for use with the standard letter in Task 80. The extra details which appear below the names and addresses will enable you to make a selective mail merge. When you have completed the datafile, print out one copy.

```
Mr R Long                         Mr G Murphy
Welsh National Bank               Valley Leisure Centre
3 Ramsey Road                     Valley Road
CARDIFF                           CARDIFF
SG2 7CD                           SG5 8DF
Pax computer                      Optima computer


Mrs P Chester                     Mr M Linwood
Financial Advisory Service Ltd    Linwood Manufacturing Ltd
16 Wood Street                    Station Road
NEWPORT                           CARDIFF
NT6 8RT                           SG3 2LB
Optima computer                   Optima computer


Ms R Powell                       Ms F Armstrong
The Preservation Co Ltd           Armstrong Antiques
26 Portside Road                  18 High Street
CARDIFF                           NEWPORT
SG2 3FK                           NT8 4WR
Pax computer                      Pax computer
```

Continued ▶

UNIT 1
SEARCH AND REPLACE

1·1 Global search and replace

The **global search and replace** facility provides a quick and reliable way of changing all references to a particular word, character or phrase throughout a document. Usually, this function allows text to be changed automatically. For example, all references to a company product in a sales brochure can be changed as soon as a new product comes on the market, while the remaining text of the sales brochure is left intact.

Before you start to key in the tasks, make notes on how to operate the global search and replace facility. (Some word processing packages may call this 'find and replace', or may even use some other term.) You can test that your notes are correct by working through Task 1. When you have done this, key your notes into a Checklist and print out a copy for future reference.

TASK 1

Key in Task 1 and proof read it carefully. Then store it on disc and print out one copy.

```
TASK 1

               ARRANGING TRAVEL AND ACCOMMODATION

It is possible to plan and book a business trip without even
leaving the office.  This can easily be done by using a
Viewdata service, such as Prestel, Ceefax or Oracle.

Viewdata is a term which describes large computer databases
which are made available to the public on television or home
computer screens.  The information contained in a Viewdata
system is accessed by making selections from appropriate
display menus until the exact information required appears on
the screen.

Travel details are easy to obtain from the Viewdata system,
and it is possible to find train and flight times for all over
the country and abroad.  Currency exchange rates, current
weather forecasts, health requirements and hotel vacancies are
also given by Viewdata.

In fact, access to a Viewdata system is essential for any
company whose executives are obliged to make frequent business
trips.  Before Viewdata became available, a great deal of time
was wasted searching through reference sources to find travel
data which is now instantly accessible.
```

Now recall Task 1 and using the global search and replace facility replace the word 'Viewdata' with the word 'Videotex'. When you have checked that this is correct, print out one copy.

▶ *Continued*

Now key in the standard letter in Task 79, inserting merge codes at the points where variable information is to be merged. (These are marked here by an asterisk.) When you have completed it, proof read it carefully, store it on disc and print out a letter to everyone on the datafile who is under 21.

TASK 79

Our ref MP/(your initials)

* (Today's date)

* (Name and address of addressee)

Dear * (Name)

Thank you for replying to the recent advertisement about our banking facilities. We have passed on your letter to your local branch manager who will be contacting you about opening an account in the near future.

Meanwhile, we enclose details of the special services we have available for young people and college students, together with a complimentary copy of our booklet 'A Brief Guide To Savings and Investing'.

I would also point out that until 31 August, we are offering a free gift pack and coach travel vouchers to anyone * (age) who opens a bank account with us. We think this will be of use to you whether you are starting work or going to College or University.

Yours sincerely

Melanie Price
Nestbank Publicity Manager

Enc.

Unit 8: Selective merging

 **TASK 2**

Key in Task 2 and proof read it carefully. Then store it on disc and print out one copy.

```
TASK 2

                    MEMORANDUM

TO   All sales executives

FROM  Marketing director          DATE (Insert today's date)

Next spring we are planning a training programme to help our
sales executives compete successfully with companies in
Europe.  All executives chosen to follow the programme will be
expected to make sure that they have attended our basic and
intermediate French language sessions and have a thorough
grasp of commercial phrases and terminology.

We have produced a special booklet to be studied carefully
before the start of the programme.  It contains essential
information about the European countries within our sales
territory, and the names, designations and addresses of
personnel to be contacted.

Detailed information about the programme will be sent out at a
later date.  It is expected that the programme will take place
in our Paris Headquarters, so all executives must ensure that
they have a valid passport and international driving licence.
A travel itinerary is being arranged, and this will include
some cultural and gastronomic visits.

The training programme will be repeated in the autumn, for the
benefit of the executives not selected in the spring.
```

Now recall Task 2 and using the global search and replace facility change the word 'programme' to 'course'. Then use the global search and replace facility again and change 'executives' to 'managers'. When you have checked that this is correct, print one copy.

Unit 1: Global search and replace

TASK 79

Prepare this datafile for use with the standard letter in Task 79. The extra details which appear below the names and addresses will enable you to make a selective mail merge. When you have completed the datafile, print out one copy.

Ms M Bishop
20 Wordsworth Street
PENZANCE
PE2 8DS
under 21

Mr J Harris
3 Rookfield Avenue
TRURO
RT3 4GB
over 21

Mr B Evans
5 College Lane
CAMBORNE
TR2 3GN
over 21

Mr P Munro
4 Cedar Road
REDRUTH
RR1 LH4
under 21

Ms J Douglas
18 Manor Lane
HELSTON
HS1 ST9
under 21

Mrs V Nuttall
31 Chesterfield Road
FALMOUTH
FM7 5TH
over 21

Continued ▶

TASK 3

The global search and replace facility can often be used to help you key in long or complex phrases. A symbol can be used instead of the difficult phrase, and when keying in is complete the symbol can easily be replaced throughout the document.

Key in Task 3 and proof read it carefully. Then store it on disc and print out one copy.

```
TASK 3


                       Your * Policy

This * Policy has been specially devised by our experts to
cover all your needs.  We are confident that the level of
protection offered in the * Policy is what you expect from us.

The * Policy is evidence that a contract has been made between
the Insurer and the Policy Holder, and you should read through
it carefully to make sure that it has fulfilled your
requirements.

The Insurer will provide insurance as described in the *
Policy for any sickness, loss or damage which may occur during
the period specified.

The full conditions and exclusions which apply to the whole of
your * Policy are contained in our booklet which will be sent
to you separately.  The booklet contains explanatory notes to
help you understand your * Policy, but these notes are not
part of the legal wording of your contract.

If for any reason, you do not find our * Policy to your
satisfaction, you may return it to us within 7 days for a full
refund of the premium paid.  In any event, should you wish to
examine the terms, conditions and exclusions of the * Policy
in advance, you may ask for a specimen copy before booking is
made.
```

Now recall Task 3 and replace '*' with 'Traveller's Insurance'. When you have checked that the document is correct, print out one copy.

Unit 1: Global search and replace

▶ Continued

Now key in the standard letter in Task 78, inserting merge codes at the points where variable information is to be merged. (These are marked here by an asterisk.) When you have completed it, proof read it carefully, store it on disc and print out a letter to everyone on the datafile who lives in Bradford.

TASK 78

Our ref MH/(your initials)

* (Today's date)

* (Name and address of addressee)

Dear * (Name)

We are offering a new range of contract cleaning services to all our long-standing customers in your area. We know that you have used our maintenance and cleaning personnel for some time now, and have been entirely satisfied with them.

For customers like yourself, we are starting to extend our services, and from the beginning of next week, in addition to our standard office cleaning contract, we are offering company window cleaning and a weekly executive car wash and wax.

Some of our customers have also enquired about the possibility of flower arrangement and plant care, and we are delighted to announce that we now employ several florists to cater for these needs.

We would be happy to discuss your individual requirements with you, and a discount of 15% is being offered to customers signing an annual agreement for any new service with us within the next six weeks.

Please do not hesitate to phone us for an informal discussion.

Yours sincerely

Max Hunter
Company Cleaning Ltd

Unit 8: Selective merging

UNIT 1
SEARCH AND REPLACE
1·2 The search facility

Although the **search** facility is used for finding particular words or phrases in a document, it does not replace them automatically each time. It enables the user to choose whether they are to be replaced or not, and allows different replacements to be made.

This is a very time-saving facility, and it also means that complete accuracy can be ensured when a piece of text has to be corrected throughout a whole document.

Before you key in Task 4, make some brief notes on how to operate the search facility. (It is sometimes called the 'find' facility.) When you are sure your notes are correct, key them into a Checklist and print out a copy for future reference.

TASK 4

Key in Task 4, using '*' where indicated. When you have finished, proof read it carefully, then store it and print out one copy.

```
TASK 4

                        MICRO WORLD LTD
                         29 YORK WAY
                       NORTHAMPTON NR6 8XD
                       Telephone 0604 22395

CONFERENCE BOOKING FORM

Kindly make the following bookings for the Desktop Publishing
Conference in October.  I agree to abide by the terms and
conditions printed on the reverse side of the Booking Form.

Name:                   *

Address:                *



Post code:              *          Telephone number:    *

CONFERENCE DETAILS

Date of attendance: * 20           Number of tickets:   *

PAYMENT

Credit card:            *          Amount:              *

Card number:            *          Expiry date:         *

Signature ....................     Date ....................
```

29+3   Continued ▶

Unit 1: The search facility

7

MAIL MERGE

8·3 Selective merging

Sometimes, it is not appropriate to send letters to everyone on a mailing list. For a variety of reasons, only some of the names and addresses may need to be targeted, so that what is required is a **selective mailshot**.

Obviously it would be a waste of time and money to print out letters to everyone on a mailing list and throw away the ones that are not required. Therefore, most mail merge facilities allow the user to select the names and addresses that are wanted.

Make notes on how your system allows you to do this, and test them out in the following task. If they are correct, key them into a Checklist for future reference.

TASK 78

Prepare this datafile for use with the standard letter in Task 78. When you have completed the datafile, print out one copy.

```
Ms J Weldon                    Mr P Cooper
Furniture World Ltd            Cooper Printers
6 Broughton Road               18 Rushdon Road
BRADFORD                       HUDDERSFIELD
BT1 6RM                        HU6 9LR


Mr J Eaton                     Mrs E Blyth
Eaton Sports Shop              Northern Electrical Ltd
2 Derwent Street               5 Park Parade
HALIFAX                        BRADFORD
HA5 6WJ                        BT2 8RZ


Mrs H Carlton                  Mr M Patel
Angels Boutique                Quick Copies Ltd
3 Raglan Street                17 Cranborn Street
HUDDERSFIELD                   BRADFORD
HU4 8BJ                        BT4 6TS
```

Continued ▶

Unit 8: Selective merging

▶ Continued

Now recall Task 4, and using the search facility go through the document to find each '*'. Replace them by keying in the information given below, remembering to delete each '*'. Print out the task when you have finished.

```
TASK 4
                        MICRO WORLD LTD
                          29 YORK WAY
                       NORTHAMPTON NR6 8XD
                       Telephone 0604 22395

CONFERENCE BOOKING FORM

Kindly make the following bookings for the Desktop Publishing
Conference in October.  I agree to abide by the terms and
conditions printed on the reverse side of the Booking Form.
```

Name: *Michael Green*

Address: *Oxford Lighting Co*
27 Western Avenue
OXFORD

Post code: *OX3 9RD*   Telephone number: *0865 72493*

CONFERENCE DETAILS

Date of attendance: *4 October*   Number of tickets: *1*

PAYMENT

Credit card: *Visa*   Amount: *£95*

Card number: *4939 8510 90*   Expiry date: *(insert next May's date)*

Signature ....   Date *(today's date)*...

Unit 1: The search facility

▶ Continued

Now key in the standard letter in Task 77, inserting merge codes at the points where variable information is to be merged. (These are marked here by an asterisk.) When you have completed it, proof read it carefully and store it on disc, then print out a copy to everyone on the datafile.

TASK 77

Our ref AL/(your initials)

* (Today's date)

* (Name and address of addressee)

Dear * (Name)

Thank you for your application of * (date). We are delighted to enclose your * (product), and welcome you as a new member of the association.

With so many different cards available, you will naturally need to be reassured that yours will be recognised in a large number of retail outlets both at home and abroad.

Our years of expertise in this field mean that we can readily offer you a guarantee that all major retailing outlets listed in our directory will recognise your card.

We are truly delighted that you have decided to become a member of our association and, as promised, we have a little surprise in store for you.

We would ask you to call in at your local branch in * (town), where, on presentation of your card, you will be given a small welcome present consisting of a set of coasters.

Yours sincerely

Subscriptions Manager

Unit 8: Merging other details

TASK 5

Key in Task 5 using '*' where indicated. When you have finished, proof read it carefully, then store it and print out one copy.

```
TASK 5

Our ref *


*


*




Dear *

*

Thank you for your application for the post of * in our *
department.

In connection with this, we would like you to attend an
interview on * at *.  Please bring with you any examination
certificates you may have.

If you are unable to attend, do ring my assistant * to let us
know.

Yours sincerely



Janet Wilson
Personnel Officer
```

Continued ▶

Unit 1: The search facility

TASK 77

Prepare this datafile for use with the standard letter in Task 77. The extra details appear below the names and addresses. Check your system to see if they can be stored in the datafile, or whether they will have to be inserted in the standard document from the keyboard. When you have completed the datafile, print out one copy.

```
Mr P Conway                    Ms S Hobart
14 College Drive               17 Grassmere Avenue
NOTTINGHAM                     MATLOCK
NH7 6GR                        MT10 8SU
20 April                       25 April
Gold Card                      Master Card
Nottingham                     Matlock


Ms D Churchill                 Mr R Gardiner
12 Byron Court                 6 Lombard Road
Parklands Road                 SURBITON
LONDON                         SN1 8TN
N13 5TY                        26 April
22 April                       Silver Card
Master Card                    Kingston
Palmers Green


Mrs J Irving                   Mr L Stratton
25 Upper Mounts                9 Windsor Road
NORTHAMPTON                    WATFORD
NN3 6BE                        Herts WD2 4RJ
23 April                       28 April
Silver Card                    Master Card
Northampton                    Watford
```

Continued ▶

Unit 8: Merging other details

▶ Continued

Now recall Task 5, and using the search facility go through the document to find each '*'. Replace them by keying in the information given below, remembering to delete each '*'. Print out the task when you have finished.

TASK 5

Our ref **PT/JW**

Today's date

Ms R Heaton
29 Chase Side
PLYMOUTH
PY4 9MH

Dear **Ms Heaton**

INTERVIEW

Thank you for your application for the post of **secretary** in our **advertising** department.

In connection with this, we would like you to attend an interview on **(insert date for a week from today)** at **2·00 pm**. Please bring with you any examination certificates you may have.

If you are unable to attend, do ring my assistant **Sue Walsh** to let us know.

Yours sincerely

Janet Wilson
Personnel Officer

Unit 1: The search facility

▶ Continued

Now key in the standard letter in Task 76, inserting merge codes at the points where variable information is to be merged. (These are marked here by an asterisk.) When you have completed it, proof read it carefully and store it on disc, then print out a copy to everyone on the datafile.

TASK 76

* (Today's date)

* (Name and address of addressee)

Dear * (Name)

Thank you for your letter of * (date of letter). We are sorry to hear that you are not fully satisfied with your new * (product).

We pride ourselves on our no-risk undertaking, and always give our customers a full thirty days to make up their minds. Every office accessory we sell should give complete satisfaction. If not, you can return it for a refund of the total price paid, less delivery charges.

As you can see, we are standing by our promise, and we enclose a cheque for * (amount) as a full refund, and hope that you will look through our brochure again and find another item to your liking.

We would call your attention to our extensive range of video equipment which is featured on pages 10 to 14. Choosing compatible systems is easy when you shop with us, as we have already selected suitable kits for you, ranging from a starter pack to a highly sophisticated system.

Do ring our hotline if you need further advice or assistance.

Yours sincerely

Whitaker Catalogues Ltd

Enc

UNIT 1

SEARCH AND REPLACE
1·3
Using prior information to replace text

Sometimes the information to be inserted in a document will not be written out for you as it has been in the previous tasks. You may be required to read through past correspondence or other documents in order to find it, and you will have to insert it in the document as you think fit.

TASK 6

Key in Task 6, using a symbol (e.g. & or *) to indicate points where text is to be entered later. Then proof read it carefully, store it and print out one copy.

```
TASK 6

              HADDON HOTEL AND CONFERENCE CENTRE
                 WEST HEATH, MATLOCK ME3 3JG

Telephone Matlock 404341                    Telex 907044 M

Delegates are advised to read carefully through the notes at
the end of the brochure before completing and signing this
form.  We wish to draw attention to the fact that special
dietary requirements must be booked in advance.

Delegate's name:   &

Address:   &



Telephone number:   &

ACCOMMODATION DETAILS

Arrival date:   &

Departure date:   &

Type of room required:   &

PAYMENT

Amount of deposit:   &



Signature ......................    Date ......................

SPECIAL REQUESTS (PLEASE SPECIFY BELOW)
```

Continued ▶

MAIL MERGE

8.2 Merging other details

The growth of the mail order industry has led to the demand for fully personalised documents. It is not sufficient just to fill in an individual's name and address on a letter. Other details also have to be changed so that the document will suit the individual's particular circumstances.

Study your word processing manual carefully to see how your system allows this to be done. It will be necessary to prepare your standard document so that the particulars can be inserted in the correct places. Make careful notes on how this is done, and try them out on the next task. If they are correct, key them into a Checklist and print out a copy for reference.

TASK 76

Prepare this datafile for use with the standard letter in Task 76. The extra details appear below the names and addresses. Check your system to see if they can be stored in the datafile, or whether they will have to be inserted in the standard document from the keyboard. When you have completed the datafile, print out one copy.

```
Miss J Brayfield              Mr L Ryan
32 Shakespeare Road           12 Hunter House
LONDON                        205 Keble Road
W6 3SJ                        LONDON
6 March                       N12 4SR
electronic typewriter         10 March
£95                           car alarm
                              £45


Mrs H Johnson                 Mr A Layzell
Flat 5                        2 Rosebank Avenue
91 Junction Road              LONDON
LONDON                        SW15 6EW
N19 5EJ                       12 March
7 March                       calculator
short wave radio              £8
£37
```

Continued ▶

▶ *Continued*

Recall Task 6 and complete the booking form with information given in the letter below. Use the search facility to find the symbol (e.g. & or *) used to mark the entry point for the information, and remember to delete the symbol when you key in the information. Print out one copy.

```
                        26 Westfield Gardens
                              SHEFFIELD
                              SH2 6LD


Haddon Hotel and Conference Centre
West Heath
MATLOCK
ME3 3JG



Dear Mr Taylor

            COMPUTER SOFTWARE CONFERENCES

Thank you for your brochure and price list about the
forthcoming series of conferences.  I would like to book
myself in for the the spreadsheet conference from 2 to 4
November.

I would prefer to have a single room with ensuite bathroom,
and will require a vegetarian diet.

I enclose my cheque for £50 for the deposit.  If there are any
problems, do not hesitate to ring me at home on 288430.

                    Yours sincerely

                    Diane Baker

                    Diane Baker (Mrs)

Enc
```

Unit 1: Using prior information to replace text

▶ Continued

Now key in the standard letter in Task 75, inserting merge codes at the points where variable information is to be merged. (These are marked here by an asterisk.) When you have completed it, proof read it carefully and store it on disc, then print out a copy to everyone on the datafile.

TASK 75

Our ref AL/(your initials)

(Today's date)

* (Name and address of addressee)

Dear * (Name)

We are writing to remind you for the second time that your account with us is overdue. It is now ten weeks since our original invoice was sent to you, and we are still awaiting payment.

We appreciate that you are a customer of many years' standing, and therefore hesitate to resort to further action. However, we are sure that you understand that we cannot operate our own business successfully unless payments are met on time.

Accordingly, we would urge you to settle your account immediately, or to contact us with a view to renegotiating your debt. Otherwise we regret that we will be obliged to take legal action.

Yours sincerely

Anne Lambert
Accounts Manager

TASK 7

Key in Task 7, using a symbol (e.g. @ or *) to indicate points where text is to be entered later. Then proof read it carefully, store it and print out one copy.

TASK 7

                               Angloworld Furniture Packs Ltd
                                    Wellington Industrial Estate
                                                 LEEDS LS12 1ET

                    Customer Complaint Form

Date Complaint Received: @

Complaints referring to damaged parts should be referred back
to the retailer. This form should only be used in connection
with complaints about a shortage of fittings, and it should be
filed with the original complaint letter/message when the
missing part(s) have been dispatched.

Type of product: @

Product finish: @

Size: height: @   width: @   depth: @

Purchased from (name of store): @

Branch: @

Item(s) missing: @   Number required: @

Continued ▶

Unit 1: Using prior information to replace text

TASK 75

Prepare this datafile for use with the standard letter in Task 75. When you have completed the datafile, print out one copy.

Mr M Jennings
Magic Moment Videos Ltd
4 High Street
DORCHESTER
DT1 1DG

Mr A Roberts
Roberts Newsagents
6 Hertford Road
HATFIELD
HA6 4TF

Mrs M Palmer
Palmer Accommodation
56 Chigwell Road
WOODFORD
DF4 7DW

Mr F Waterland
Charterhouse Finance Ltd
19 Eastern Avenue
SUNDERLAND
SU3 2NF

Continued ▶

▶ *Continued*

Recall Task 7 and complete the customer complaint form with the information given in the telephone message below. Use the search facility to find the symbol (e.g. @ or *) used to mark the entry point for the information, and remember to delete the symbol when you key in the information. Print out one copy.

TELEPHONE MESSAGE

Name of caller: **Mrs Jones**　　　　　Phone no: **081-935 7668**

Address: **27 Farm Walk**
Isleworth
Middx   TW7 5AD

Message: **3 drawer white melamine chest – H 590 mm W 500 mm D 395 mm – purchased from Dallas Stores, Twickenham – only 2 drawer handles enclosed.**

Message taken by: **Jackie**

Date: **20 September**　　　　　Time: **2.30 pm.**

▶ *Continued*

Now key in the standard letter in Task 74, inserting merge codes at the points where variable information is to be merged. (These are marked here by an asterisk.) When you have completed it, proof read it carefully and store it on disc. Then print out a copy to everyone on the datafile.

TASK 74

(Today's date)

* (Name and address of addressee)

Dear * (Name)

We are writing to tell you about our exclusive new service for all credit card holders. TELESHOPPER is a telephone shopping service which helps you make substantial savings on thousands of household items, leisure goods and consumer durables.

Whether you want to buy a jar of coffee, a badminton racket or a new washing machine, just pick up the phone and you will be given the latest information and the lowest prices in Britain. The service also enables you to purchase the item using your credit card, and arranges delivery to your door.

You are invited to join TELESHOPPER free of charge for a trial period of three months. Just complete and return the attached form – you have nothing to lose, so why not join now?

There really is something for everyone in TELESHOPPER, and we promise that all our goods are offered for sale at 25% or more off the manufacturer's recommended retail price. Whether you are buying for your own use or for your family, we promise that you will make truly incredible savings.

When you start to shop with us, we will send you our free monthly magazine. It is full of tips and advice and reviews several new products on the market each month. We always include several coupons to help you make even greater savings, and there is always at least one competition to enter with a superb prize for the lucky winner.

Yours sincerely

Andrew McDonald
TELESHOPPER SERVICES

TASK 8

Key in Task 8, using a symbol (e.g. @ or *) to indicate points where text is to be entered later. Then proof read it carefully, store it and print out one copy.

TASK 8

BROOKSIDE MANUFACTURING LIMITED
HINCKLEY
OXON BT6 9HV

Software Order Form

Members of staff must discuss their requirements with their departmental manager before ordering software, and an authorisation signed by a departmental manager must accompany any requests.

Name of software package: @

Manufacturer: @   Version: @

Distributor's name and address: @

Number of copies required: @

Cost per package: @   Total cost: @

Member of staff placing order: @

Department: @

Date: @

Continued ▶

Unit 1: Using prior information to replace text

TASK 74

Prepare this datafile for use with the standard letter in Task 74. When you have completed the datafile, print out one copy.

```
Mrs B Kennedy                    Mr   J Erskine
1 The Avenue                     32 Cedar Road
MARLBOROUGH                      RAMSGATE
SN8 7DA                          RM5 3YE


Ms R Lewis                       Mr W Coleman
Flat 10                          18 Radcliff Gardens
19 Milton Street                 WINCHESTER
PLYMOUTH                         SO7 2JX
PT8 SM4


Mr D Barber                      Ms B Taylor
Flat 2                           1 Wellgarth Road
45 Bridge Street                 SOUTHAMPTON
PORTSMOUTH                       SS3 3BE
PR1 2ST
```

Continued ▶

Continued ▶

Recall Task 8 and complete the software order form with the information given in the memorandum below. Use the search facility to find the symbol (e.g. @ or *) used to mark the entry point for the information, and remember to delete the symbol when you key in the information. Print out one copy.

MEMORANDUM

TO   The Purchasing Manager

FROM   Mark Wood, Design Department   DATE 3 October

As you know, the Design Department relies heavily on a wide variety of computer techniques, and the demand is always increasing. Consequently, I have obtained written authorisation from the departmental manager to order some new software packages which are priced at £399 per copy.

Unfortunately, I have run out of order forms, and as my department is based in the annexe, I have not managed to call round to the main building to collect some more. I am therefore sending you this (together with the written authorisation to order "Desktop Design" version 2.1) via the internal mail system, and I wonder if you could send me back some more forms in the same way.

What I require is 3 copies. The manufacturer is Digisoft, who as you may remember, produced the last package we ordered. The software is distributed by the Cambridge Computer Corporation, Unit 5, River Bank Industrial Park, Cambridge CB2 5RE.

Enc

Unit 1: Using prior information to replace text

▶ Continued

Now key in the standard letter in Task 73, inserting merge codes at the points where variable information is to be merged. (These are marked here by an asterisk.) When you have completed it, proof read it carefully and store it on disc. Then print out a copy to everyone on the datafile.

TASK 73

Our ref MR/(your initials)

(Today's date)

* (Name and address of addressee)

Dear * (Name)

Thank you for your recent enquiry about our latest office equipment. I enclose a brochure which gives detailed information about our full range of products and incorporates a price list.

If you would like a demonstration of any of our products, this can be done informally by calling in at our central showroom. Alternatively, you can make a prior booking, or we may be able to send a representative to your premises.

You can be confident that if you choose one of our office systems, you will get complete reliability and sophisticated performance. Our new range of equipment is more compact and streamlined than ever before, as we aim to provide you with more processing power using less desk space.

Each system has been specially designed to meet the latest requirements in office technology. We continue to offer compatibility, flexibility and perfect performance together with an unrivalled pricing policy.

Do not hesitate to telephone us if you need further information or would like to discuss your specific requirements with us. We undertake to provide a quotation, no matter how complex, within five working days.

Yours sincerely

Michelle Ross
Sales Manager

Enc

Unit 8: Merging names and addresses in standard letters

TASK 9

In this task you will be expected to perform a global search and replace and also make alterations using the search facility. First key in Task 9 and proof read it carefully. Then store it on disc and print out one copy.

TASK 9

(Insert today's date)

Mr S Turner
Turner and Newall Ltd
22 Westfield Lane
NOTTINGHAM
NN3 7HA

Dear Mr Turner

Thank you for your enquiry about the Communications Symposium. Below is a summary of the events for the four days.

DAY 1 Arrival and registration. At the morning session, there will be a talk about the current state of research into satellite transmission and the part the micro is playing in this. The afternoon session will consist of a video presentation of the latest satellite launch and a discussion of the problems encountered.

DAY 2 The advantages of this new form of communication will be outlined - in particular, the effects it will have on micro owners and on television wave lengths.

DAY 3 The emphasis today will be on micro links and the transmission of database information on a global scale. There will be demonstrations of the current micro links, and television videotex services.

DAY 4 The micro will be the main topic for today, and there will be a display of the hardware on the market which makes long-range links possible. Delegates will also be able to try out the different software packages available with a view to choosing a suitable one for the particular applications of their own micro.

Yours sincerely

Now recall Task 9 and using the global search and replace facility change 'micro' to 'computer'. Then, using the search facility, alter DAY 1 to MONDAY, DAY 2 to TUESDAY, DAY 3 to WEDNESDAY and DAY 4 to THURSDAY. When you have checked that the document is correct, print out one copy.

Unit 1: Using prior information to replace text

UNIT 8

MAIL MERGE

8·1 Merging names and addresses in standard letters

Mail merge, or print merge as it is sometimes called, is a very useful device which enables personalised letters to be sent out to a large number of different people. A personalised letter will contain the name and address of the individual to whom it is sent, and will also include the individual's name in the salutation.

To do this, a standard letter has to be prepared and stored on disc. This letter will contain 'merge codes' at the places where variable information is to be inserted. This means 'merge codes' must be keyed in where the name and address of the addressee are to be printed and also in the salutation after the word 'Dear'. It may also be possible to use a 'merge code' for keying in the current date.

A datafile which contains the variable information must also be prepared. This information consists of the names and addresses of the people who are to receive the standard letter. 'Merge codes' are included in this document too, otherwise it would merely be a mailing list which could not be incorporated in the standard letter.

Make careful notes about setting up a standard document and a datafile, and test them in the following tasks. You will also need to make notes on how to merge the standard document with the variable information – and whether you will see the results on screen, or only at the print stage. If all your notes are correct, key them into a Checklist and print out a copy for future reference.

TASK 73

Prepare this datafile for use with the standard letter in Task 73. When you have completed the datafile, print out one copy.

```
Mr T Patterson              Mr J Clarke
Patterson and Leigh         Moonlight Jewellers
Estate Agents               8 Queens Parade
9 Market Place              NORWICH
KINGSTON                    SR3 6ND
KT5 8GN


Mrs J Marsh                 Mr A Baker
Transit Travel              Golden Gate Photographers
9 Inverness Gardens         3 New Road
LIVERPOOL                   WINDSOR
L8 7PR                      SL5 4DS
```

Continued ▶

TASK 10

This is a timed task which should take you no longer than 30 minutes to complete and print out.

In this task you will be expected to perform a global search and replace and also make alterations using the search facility. First key in Task 10, store it on disc and print out one copy. Then complete the amendments and print out another copy.

```
TASK 10


                    PC USERS' CLUB NEWSLETTER

                       MEETINGS IN NOVEMBER

Monday 6

Bring your PC along to this meeting as we are going to examine
all the software available for playing the latest computer
games.  You cannot join in if you have not got your own PC!
You will just have to sit back and spectate.

Monday 13

This evening we shall be discussing the latest books and
software available for programming on the PC.  Come and bring
your own software and give your recommendations.

Monday 20

PC users' party night.  Please bring a bottle.  A small
contribution will be required to pay for the food.  We are
leaving the serious world of PC software and hardware behind
and going to enjoy ourselves.

Monday 27

We are back tonight to listen to advice about the dreadful
problem of the corrupted disc.  Disc Doctor Ron Smith is going
to talk to us about disc care and back-up procedures for the
PC.  He also does disc salvage work, so if your disc dies on
you, do not despair, help is at hand.
```

Change PC to Amstrad throughout the newsletter and alter the dates, as many people find Monday inconvenient.

Monday 6 becomes Tuesday 7
Monday 13 becomes Thursday 16
Monday 20 becomes Friday 24
Monday 27 becomes Wednesday 29

Unit 1: Using prior information to replace text

TASK 72

This is a timed task which should take you no longer than 20 minutes to complete and print out.

Key in Task 72, making amendments as indicated. When you have completed it, proof read it carefully and print out one copy.

TASK 72

COMPUTER SECURITY

PASSWORDS

Passwords are used to limit the number of people using a computer system and how much access they have. However, it is amazing how difficult it is to invent an original password, and how people naïvely use the most obvious words.

Words like 'help', 'test', 'system', 'terminal', 'operations', 'remote', 'network' and 'Fred' turn up over and over again. It is often easy to guess passwords if you know something about the company or the occupation of the password holder. It would not be at all surprising to find one of the Water Boards using H₂O as a password, or an opera lover using Aïda. The repertoire of passwords in common use is very limited.

SECURITY CONSULTANTS

The number of computer security experts is increasing. What they try to do is to divide up the responsibility for the computer system as much as they can. For example, only programmers can access the operating system, only systems managers can validate passwords, and only operators can touch the physical installation.

The next step is to make sure a surveillance program is available to record and monitor who accesses the system. Separate programs can also test if one terminal is getting more use than another, or if unsuccessful attempts are being made to log on and where this is happening.

Of course, the crème de la crème of British companies will be able to purchase installations where security is already built into the operating system. However, experience has shown that security systems are not often used properly, and fraudsters have been phenomenally successful.

Embolden the main heading and put all examples of passwords in bold instead of inverted commas. Hyphenate words at line ends if necessary.

Unit 7: Special characters and hyphenation

UNIT 2

PAGINATION

2.1 Page breaks

A long document must be split up into pages, as it is not possible to print it out on a single sheet of paper. Most word processing systems display on the screen the number of lines there are on the page and give some indication when the last line has been reached. However, it is possible to end a page wherever you want by inserting a **page break**. (This is called 'forcing a page'.) A page break is an instruction to the printer to start printing out on a fresh sheet of paper.

Before you start to key in Task 11, make notes on how to insert a page break, and make sure you know how many lines there are in a page and can see the number of the line your cursor is on. By completing the task you can make sure that your notes are correct, and if they are you can key them into a Checklist and keep them for future reference.

TASK 11

Key in Task 11 using single line spacing and margins of one and a half inches. Your system may insert a page break, but if not you can force a page where necessary. When you have finished, proof read it carefully, store it on disc, then print out one copy.

TASK 11

USING THE TELEPHONE SYSTEM TO THE FULL

Telephone lines are not just for conversations, though this is what most people use them for. Every busy office has a trained telephonist whose job it is to answer the phone and connect callers to the person with whom they wish to speak. However, there are many other uses for telephone lines which are just as important as transmitting conversations.

When linked to a computer, the telephone line can be put to other uses. Here are some examples of the sort of ways in which it can be used.

*   Businesses can access information instantly. This could
        be stock market prices, travel news, weather forecasts or
        details held on databases concerning customers or other
        firms.

*   Telexes can be prepared and sent using the word
        processing facilities of the computer. This is
        especially useful for small businesses which cannot
        afford the rental or purchase price of a telex machine.

Continued ▶

TASK 71

Key in Task 71, making amendments where indicated. When you have completed it, proof read it carefully and print out one copy.

TASK 71

HOW DANGER STRIKES

'Office safety' is not just about sitting in a room where the temperature has reached at least 16°C, where there are 3.7m² of space per person and crèche facilities for children. It also covers the business of computer security.

As most offices are now computerised, the safety of the computer and its discs is of major importance. There are many disasters that may strike.

The Deadly Virus

A virus is a program which disables a computer system, usually by attacking its hard disc, so that work stored on floppies from the hard disc will also be infected and may in turn infect other computer systems. Viruses spread fast. Two infected discs can soon ruin 2¹⁰ discs.

Corrupted Discs

A disc is corrupted when the magnetic fields recorded on it are damaged. This could be by allowing heat, liquid or dirt, to touch the disc, by putting it near a telephone or magnet, or by a slight misalignment in the heads that read the disc. To make a précis of all the advice about how to care for your discs, one could just say: take good care of them and always make back-up copies.

The Dreaded Hacker

A brief résumé of the history of hacking will show that the term has changed from meaning simply a computer enthusiast to meaning a potential criminal who makes illegal entry into other people's computer systems.

Embolden all headings and hyphenate words at line ends if necessary

---

Unit 7: Special characters and hyphenation

▶ *Continued*

* Employees can access their own company's mainframe computer for information, using the computer merely as a terminal.

* Documents can be sent to any part of the country without having to print them out.

* The normal postal system can be completely avoided, and so can all the problems associated with it. The computerised system of sending post is called electronic mail.

Firms, especially small ones, often wonder if a communications link will really benefit them. Here are some points to bear in mind.

1) Electronic mail is obviously useful as a quick means of communication if customers and suppliers are already subscribers to the electronic mail network.

2) The massive databases available provide essential business information instantly.

3) This information is usually about the credit status of companies or individuals, or about trading opportunities or market research. Access to it may be essential to allow a company to operate successfully.

4) Popular information services, like Prestel, may save a lot of time and trouble whenever general information is required, such as currency exchange rates, or airline travel data.

5) This sort of computer link will undoubtedly become more common as time goes by. It would be wise to start learning about it as soon as possible.

6) Competitors are probably already linked up to the world of 'on-line information services'. By not joining them now, a company may not be around to join them later.

When you have printed out Task 11 in single line spacing, recall it and alter the spacing to double line, changing the page breaks where necessary. Print it out again.

TASK 69

Key in Task 69, using hyphens to divide words at line ends if necessary. When you have completed it, proof read it carefully and print out one copy.

TASK 69

Most English words are not very long. However, there are many exceptions to this. If you stop to think, words like encyclopaedia soon spring to mind. A search through a dictionary soon reveals many other words with more than ten letters, like multimillionaire, accommodation, correspondence, disproportionate, overbalance, qualification and superintendent.

Technical passages often have long words that could be hyphenated. A short passage about word processing may use terms like subscript, superscript, highlighting, amendments to text, boilerplating, consolidation exercises, insertions, deletions and justification.

If any of these words, or any other long word, comes at the end of a line, it is advisable to divide it up by inserting a hyphen. Otherwise, a big gap may be left. When text containing long words is justified, wide spaces will be left between words unless hyphens are used.

TASK 70

Key in Task 70, using hyphens to divide words at line ends if necessary. When you have completed it, proof read it carefully and print out one copy with a justified right-hand margin.

TASK 70

Whenever a new invention increases automation and industrialisation, there are always many people who oppose it because it threatens their employment prospects. This is often puzzling to the inventor, who naturally views this attitude as backwardness or foolishness and cannot understand why there is such opposition to technological advance.

The long strike in the newspaper industry caused by the implementation of computerisation is a good example of the bitterness and confrontation that can arise when substantial change is introduced to established working practices. The employers were suddenly regarded as untrustworthy and deceitful by their workforce, who demonstrated violently against them. They may indeed have been guilty of misjudgement, and may have underestimated the effects of introducing automation.

TASK 12

Key in Task 12 using double line spacing and margins of one and a half inches. Your system may insert page breaks, but if not you can force a page where necessary. When you have finished, proof read it carefully, store it, then print out one copy.

TASK 12

Electronic Mail

This service enables a subscriber to send messages electronically using the phone lines. The messages are stored until they are retrieved by their intended recipients. Advantages of the system are:

1) Unlike using the telephone, the person you want to contact does not have to be in when you call. This is very useful for busy managers who are seldom at their desks and may miss urgent messages or have to face the anger of a caller who has tried to contact them in vain several times before.

2) The message is in the form of a text file and provides a permanent record, unlike words over the telephone which can be misheard or quickly forgotten.

3) As the message is in the form of text, it has the clarity of a letter, and the service is a useful and speedy way of sending complex or technically worded documents.

Continued ▶

TASK 68

Key in Task 68, using foreign characters where shown. When you have completed it, proof read it carefully and print out one copy.

TASK 68

Marie ROUSSEAU   Marseille, le 5 février
66 rue des Misérables
13-MARSEILLE

                                        Monsieur le Directeur
                                        Laboratoire Central
                                        8 rue de Gambetta
                                        75-PARIS 14e

Monsieur le Directeur

J'ai lu dans les petites annonces du journal 'Gazette de
Paris' que vous recherchez une secrétaire qui parle anglais et
français.

Ce poste m'intéresse beaucoup et je vous prie de bien vouloir
trouver ci-joint mon curriculum vitae.

J'ai cinq ans d'expérience et je lis, écris et parle
couramment le français et l'anglais. Monsieur Molière, pour
qui je travaille jusqu'à présent, vous donnera tous les
renseignements que vous pourriez lui demander à mon sujet.

Veuillez agréer, Monsieur le Directeur, l'expression de mes
sentiments dévoués.

Marie Rousseau

Unit 7: Special characters and hyphenation

▶ *Continued*

4) It enables precise deadlines to be met more easily than relying on the postal services, and it allows immediate answers or advice to be given in complex situations.

5) People who are on the move, like journalists or salesmen, can send back reports or orders each day, simply by keying the information into a laptop computer and transmitting it with a modem. They do not have to be anywhere near their office.

Telecom Gold

Nearly every company which uses electronic mail uses Telecom Gold, the service run by British Telecom. In the late 1980s, the service had approximately 80,000 users, which gives some idea of its popularity.

Subscribers are given a numbered 'mailbox', and must quote this number whenever they dial in. Obviously, messages can only be sent to others who are registered users of Telecom Gold, and this is done by quoting their mailbox numbers. They will be told that a message is waiting for them when they next dial in.

Many additional services have also been built up, both for business users and for home computer enthusiasts.

Continued ▶

UNIT 7 STYLE

7·4 Special characters and hyphenation

Many word processors have additional facilities which enable them to print documents using foreign characters or special symbols. In addition, some allow text to be refined by hyphenating long words at line-ends so that large gaps in the text are not caused.

If your word processor uses a daisy wheel printer, it is unlikely that many special characters can be printed out without changing the daisy wheel. Look through your manual to see what your system allows.

The following tasks will give examples of French, German and Spanish characters and hyphens at line-ends. Make notes on how these characters are produced, and when you have made sure that your notes are correct key them into a Checklist for future reference.

TASK 67

Key in Task 67, using foreign characters where shown. When you have completed it, proof read it carefully and print out one copy.

TASK 67

Acute accent - this is a forward-sloping mark over a vowel, as over the e in 'café' (French), and the o in 'Miró', the i in 'país' and the a in 'sábado' (Spanish).

Grave accent - this is a backward-sloping mark over a vowel, as in 'à la carte' (French).

Circumflex accent - this is the mark over a vowel which looks a little bit like a hat, as in 'fête' (French).

Cedilla - this is the mark written under the letter c in certain languages to show it is pronounced like an s, as in 'français' (French).

Diaeresis - this is a mark placed over a vowel to show it is sounded separately, as in 'naïve'. In German this sign is known as the umlaut, and it is used in many German words such as 'Käse', 'Löffel' and 'grün'.

Tilde - this is a mark placed over an n in Spanish to indicate that it should be pronounced like the ny in canyon, as in 'señor' and 'mañana'.

▶ *Continued*

1) There are links (or gateways) to large-scale information banks which can provide such information as financial data and world news reports.

2) Telexes can be sent anywhere in the world to any firm that has receiving equipment.

3) Other services are available, such as foreign language translation, ticket reservations and weather reports.

4) A cheaper service called Microlink is available for the home computer user. This operates like a club and provides notice boards for messages and questions.

There are three basic charges for electronic mail services:

Registration fee

Standing charge

Connection charge (for use of the phone line).

However, other charges may be made, such as for use of the telex facility and access to specialised information via the gateway.

When you have printed out Task 12 in double line spacing, recall it and alter the spacing to single line, changing the page breaks where necessary. Print it out again.

TASK 66

Key in Task 66, using superscripts where shown. When you have completed it, proof read it carefully and print out one copy using double line spacing.

TASK 66

Physical Conditions at Work

In order to provide a safe environment at work, all premises must be kept clean. This means that the floors must be cleaned at least once a week.

To prevent overcrowding, there must be a minimum of 3.715m^2 (approximately 40 ft^2) of floor space per person, but this includes space for furniture and equipment.

A steady temperature must be maintained wherever employees have to work. The very minumum it should be is 16°C (that is 60.8°F), and at no time after the first hour of work should it fall below that.

Suitable conveniences and washing facilities accessible to all employees should be provided, as should running hot and cold water, soap and clean towels.

PAGINATION

2·2 Beginnings and endings of pages

Care must be taken in multipage documents to end a page in a sensible place. For example, it is not sensible to key in a heading at the bottom of one page and put the paragraph that follows it on the next page.

It is also unwise to split a paragraph so that a single line is left at either the bottom or the top of a page. The technical term for this is 'widows and orphans', a 'widow' being a single line left at the bottom of a page, and an 'orphan' being a single line left at the top of a page.

Multipage documents must also be numbered from the second page onwards. This can be done automatically by using headers and footers, as you will learn in the next unit, but for short documents it is usually quicker and easier to key in the page numbers at the top of the pages. You will be expected to do this in the following tasks.

TASK 13

Key in Task 13 using single line spacing and margins of one and a half inches and one inch. Your system may insert a page break, but if not you can force a page where necessary. Remember to number the pages and to avoid leaving widows and orphans. When you have finished, proof read it carefully, store it on disc, then print out one copy.

When you have printed out Task 13 in single line spacing, recall it and alter the spacing to double line, changing the page breaks where necessary. Then print it out again.

TASK 13

                    Prestel

Prestel is another main communications network, but unlike Telecom Gold it is not simply a service designed for the transfer of text. It works rather like Ceefax and Oracle on the television, and presents information page by page in a well designed form. In order to use it, it is necessary to become a subscriber, and because it is transmitted over the public telephone system, there is the additional cost of telephone bills, which may be considerable.

This service used to be known as 'Viewdata', which was a term invented in the early seventies by the British Post Office. It was used to describe an information service stored on a computer system which was accessible to anyone who had a telephone and a television set. Since then, other countries have designed their own systems or signed agreements to use the British Telecom system, Prestel, so 'Viewdata' is now just a general term for this type of service.

Continued ▶

TASK 65

Key in Task 65, using superscripts where shown. When you have completed it, proof read it carefully and print out one copy using double line spacing.

TASK 65

Superscripts

Superscripts are characters printed above the normal line. They are commonly used in measurements, such as square inches (in^2), square feet (ft^2), square centimetres (cm^2) and square metres (m^2).

Another frequent use is in mathematical equations, such as:

$x = a^2 + b^3 - c^4$

Lastly, a superscript can be used for the degree sign, as in 98.4°F and 36.9°C. However, the degree sign is sometimes made by using a special character on the keyboard, and not by using a superscript at all, so check this in your WP manual.

▶ *Continued*

Prestel provides screenfuls of information, called 'frames', but this is of a very general nature, as the service does not give entry into specialised databases. It does, however, allow the user to enter data as well as receive it, and to specify exactly what information is required.

The sort of information that Prestel provides for those who subscribe to it is:

share prices

ticket availability

travel data

weather information

sports scores.

If you are not a travel agent, you may find that this sort of information is of little use to your business. You may not find a commercial use for it, and may think of it in terms of a hobby rather than a business tool.

Another important drawback is that it is virtually impossible to transfer the information provided in the frames into a text file which can be used later. This means that you cannot incorporate it in your own documents or edit it for company use. Prestel may, therefore, be of little help to the serious business user.

Ceefax and Oracle

The UK television companies have also developed their own information services which are generally known as 'Teletext'. The BBC's service is called Ceefax and ITV's is called Oracle. However, the distinction between 'Viewdata' and 'Teletext' is getting blurred, and both types of service are often referred to as 'Videotex'.

Ceefax and Oracle are not transmitted over the public telephone network, but use television signals. They are sent directly to specially adapted television sets, which are used as visual display units to receive this information.

Apart from the different methods of transmission, they are very similar to Prestel, though of course a list of the day's television programmes is also included. The major advantages over Prestel are that Ceefax and Oracle are instantly available to all television viewers who have the correct type of set, and they do not incur large telephone bills!

Unit 2: Beginnings and endings of pages

UNIT 7

STYLE

7.3 Subscripts and superscripts

A **subscript** is a character which is printed out below the normal line, and a **superscript** is a character which is printed out above the normal line. It is unlikely that they will appear in these positions on the screen. Your word processing system will probably display them on the normal line, with a code before and after them which will act as an instruction to the printer to adjust their position.

Make notes on how to key in subscripts and superscripts (which may occasionally be referred to as superior and inferior characters). When you are confident that your notes are correct, key them into a Checklist for future reference.

TASK 64

Key in Task 64, using subscripts where shown. When you have completed it, proof read it carefully and print out one copy using double line spacing.

TASK 64

Subscripts

Subscripts are seldom used except in chemical and mathematical formulae. However, if you work in a college or university, you are likely to come across them. Here are some examples:

The formula for sulphuric acid is H_2SO_4. The formula for sugar is $C_{12}H_{22}O_{11}$. The formula for water is H_2O.

An example of a mathematical formula using subscripts is given below. It is a very complex example, but unfortunately many mathematical formulae are long and complicated.

$$Z = c_1x_1 + c_2x_2 + \ldots + c_nx_n$$

TASK 14

Key in Task 14, incorporating the amendments shown and using one and a half line spacing and margins of one and a half inches and one inch. Your system may insert a page break, but if not you can force a page where necessary. Remember to number the pages and to avoid leaving widows and orphans. When you have finished, proof read it carefully, then print out one copy.

TASK 14

DRAFT

MEMORANDUM

FROM   The Secretary, North London Small Business Club

TO   All members of the North London Small Business Club   DATE   (Insert today's date)

Following the talk given by a local computer communications specialist last Thursday evening, I have asked for some guidelines to help you link into the telephone network and to help you use your own personal computer systems effectively.

Many of us feel that our competitors are getting the better of us, and instant access to statistics and other forms of business information would be of great assistance. Here are some instructions to help you log into the electronic mail system.

TELEPHONE LINKS

As no business operates without a telephone, and the majority have at least one computer at their disposal, it is a simple matter to send and receive information by computer using the telephone network.

A Modem

This is an essential piece of equipment. It is a device which plugs into the phone socket at one end, and the computer's

Continued ▶

Unit 2: Beginnings and endings of pages

TASK 63

Key in Task 63, using 12 pitch. When you have completed it, proof read it carefully, store it and print out one copy. Then recall it, alter the pitch and print out another copy.

TASK 63

Preventing Accidents in the Office

The concept of the 'paper-less office' in which there is only hi-tech machinery, such as microcomputers, has not yet become a reality. Offices still have a lot of traditional equipment which could cause injury unless handled sensibly. Here are some recommendations for the prevention of accidents.

1. Switch off and unplug electrical equipment when not in use, or when it is necessary to open it up.

2. Read the manufacturer's instructions carefully before operating new machinery, or insist on being trained in how to use it.

3. Make sure that electrical appliances are properly wired, with the correct fuse fitted, before using them. Also ensure that they are not overloading the system.

4. Take care when opening the drawers of filing cabinets. A heavy top drawer may cause the cabinet to topple over, as may opening all the drawers together.

5. Keep gangways clear so people can pass freely without tripping.

6. Never stand on a chair to reach high objects. There is a danger not only of falling off, but also of dropping the object on someone's head.

7. Take care when lifting heavy objects. This is a frequent cause of back strain.

8. Treat fire practices seriously, as one day there may be a real emergency.

▶ *Continued*

serial socket at the other, thus linking the two together. It converts the computer's digital signals into analogue form, so that they can be transmitted over the telephone network.

A Communications Software Package

It is necessary to purchase one of the packages on the market, as these provide the instructions for sending and receiving data on disc via the modem and the telephone network.

Membership of an Electronic Information Service

There is no point having the modem and the software without being a registered ~~user of~~ *subscriber to* an information service. Without it you will not be able to access the information services – except illegally. 'Hacking', as this is known, can be a criminal offence, especially if it is done with the purpose of evading subscription charges, or if information is stolen, damaged or destroyed by the hacker.

The Problem of Poor Phone Lines

All of us know the frustration of getting ~~squeaks and grunts~~ *unfamiliar noises* on the telephone lines instead of the crystal clear reception we expected. The quality of the connection is obviously very important when (sending or receiving) data. A click or crossed line can completely ruin the information being sent.

However, this problem is overcome by communications protocols. Long files are broken up into manageable sections and transmitted in this way. Each section is checked as it is received and before the next ~~section~~ *one* is sent out. The receiving computer will report that everything is all right before the next part is transmitted. In this way, the file will be sent out and received in perfect condition.

Continued ▶

TASK 62

Key in Task 62, changing the pitch after each paragraph. If possible, use a different pitch every time. When you have completed it, proof read it carefully and print out one copy.

```
TASK 62

Making the Work Environment Safe

Safety at work is not just the responsibility of the employer.
All employees are obliged by law to take reasonable steps to
ensure their own health and safety and that of their
colleagues.  This means co-operating with employers or
supervisors to make work premises safe.

If equipment is not thought to be safe, employees must point
this out and insist that steps are taken to remedy the
situation.  They should also make sure that they have received
instruction and training in safe practices, if this applies.

Employees must refrain from misusing or interfering with
anything provided for their own health and safety or that of
others such as fire doors.  They share the task of creating a
secure working environment with their employers, and this
means that they must be especially careful and vigilant.

Office workers are also obliged to take care if they visit
other parts of the organisation, such as the factory.  They
must be conscious that there may be risks attached, such as
the dangers involved wherever heavy machinery is used, and
they must do their best to avoid accidents or injury.
```

▶ Continued

VIRUS PREVENTION ⟶ (centre)

Unfortunately, the spread of computer viruses means that we have to be extra vigilant to protect our computers from penetration. A sensible precaution is never to use software from unknown sources. This means that the only software that can ever be run is that produced and guaranteed by a reputable company. The use of free demonstration discs, shareware, public domain ^software and software downloaded by modem from bulletin boards is strongly discouraged.

User Awareness

All your employees should be aware that the use of unauthorised software, such as games and demonstration discs, can provide an easy method of virus penetration which can cause ~~serious~~ extensive damage to your company. Leaflets, posters and demonstrations should be used to impress on your employees the havoc and financial loss that viruses can cause.

Effective Protection

The best way of preventing a virus attack is to limit the number of users who have access to the computer system, and never to use discs from ~~other~~ unknown sources. The only programs that should ever be used are those from reputable outlets, and their discs will normally be supplied in sealed packages to ensure that no other person has had access to them. No company computer should ever run any other sort of software.

Detection

Every organisation must have an effective way of detecting a virus before its ill-effects become extensive. An anti-virus software package is essential, but it is necessary to know the limitations of ~~the software~~ this before installing it.

UNIT 7 STYLE

7.2 Pitch

Most word processing systems allow you to change the **character pitch** when you print out. The most commonly used character pitches are Elite (12 characters to the inch) and Pica (10 characters to the inch). Many systems also allow you to print with 15 characters to the inch.

Find out what size character pitch your word processor will allow you to use when printing out, and whether this information is displayed on screen or in a special menu. Then make brief notes on how to alter the pitch. When you are satisfied that these are correct, key them into a Checklist.

TASK 61

Recall Task 60 and alter the pitch, then print out one copy. The example below shows 15 pitch.

TASK ~~60~~ 61

JOB SATISFACTION

Psychologists believe that a job must be carefully designed, or workers will become dissatisfied and bored. When a job is designed, certain factors have to be taken into consideration:

Content

The job must provide variety and be reasonably mentally demanding Otherwise, the worker will feel like a robot and pay little attention.

Decision-making

The worker must have control over some area of decision-making. This could be the order in which work is done, or the speed, or even the way in which it is done.

Recognition

Even the most junior member of staff must receive some recognition for the job being done. This should not be patronising, however menial the job is.

Learning

Every job must offer some potential for learning. This means that staff training should be introduced to help workers reach their true potential.

Future Prospects

The job should offer some prospect of a desirable future. This does not necessarily mean promotion - it could mean greater freedom or choice.

UNIT 2 PAGINATION

2·3 Setting a page length

On most word processor systems, the page length is already set. This means it has already been decided how many lines of text can be keyed in on one page. Usually, fifty-four lines of text can be keyed in and printed on a sheet of A4 paper. There is seldom any need to change the page length, but make sure that you know how to check the length and exactly which line of the page your cursor is on.

TASK 15

Key in Task 15, incorporating the amendments shown and using double line spacing and margins of one and a half inches. Your system may insert a page break, but if not you can force a page where necessary. Remember to number the pages and to avoid leaving widows and orphans. When you have finished, proof read it carefully, then print out one copy.

TASK 15

(Insert today's date here)

TECHNOLOGICAL UPDATE

As a result of the Managing Director's recent visit to the Electronic Communications Show in ~~Tokyo~~ California, we have learned that technological advances mean that the car radio ~~set~~ will be radically changed in the very near future.

In addition, the freedom given to broadcasting is going to mean many more stations and services. This will have a big impact on the car radios we usually install in our British-made vehicles.

Several advances have already taken place in Japan and in Europe, and we can now see more clearly what the new developments are.

Continued ▶

TASK 60

Key in Task 60, amending it as indicated. When you have completed it, proof read it carefully, store it on disc and print out one copy.

TASK 60

(Embolden the main heading and side headings)

JOB SATISFACTION *(centre)*

Psychologists believe that a job must be carefully designed, or workers will become bored and dissatisfied. When a job is designed, certain factors have to be taken into consideration:

Content

The job must provide variety and be reasonably mentally demanding. Otherwise, the worker will feel like a robot and pay little attention.

Decision-making

The worker must have control over some area of decision-making. This could be the order in which work is done, or the speed, or even the way in which it is done.

Future prospects

The job should offer some prospect of a desirable future. This does not necessarily mean promotion — it could mean greater freedom or choice.

Recognition

Even the newest member of staff must receive some recognition for the job being done. This should not be patronising, however menial the job is.

Learning

Every job must offer some potential for learning. This means that staff training should be introduced to help workers reach their true potential.

▶ Continued

1) A liquid crystal display in full colour is replacing all the old-fashioned knobs and dials ∧ on the dashboard. Tuning and volume adjustment are now by touch-sensitive keys.

2) The selection of the required station is also by means of these keys, which will automatically tune into the strongest signal available for the station selected.

3) The type of programme ~~required~~ desired can be selected by touching another set of keys. For example, if pop music is required, by touching the pop music key, the radio will be tuned into the nearest pop music channel.

4) A voice synthesiser will translate foreign language bulletins into English, so that if the weather forecast key has been selected while driving in France, any weather news will be relayed to the driver in English. Other countries will have the same facilities for translating into their own languages.

5) The days when the aerial was a metal rod sticking out from the side of the car will soon be over, and so will the risk of detection and vandalism. It is planned to make the new aerial consist of a small panel in the roof of the car which is painted to match. No-one will even be able to tell it is there, and it will be impossible to break it off.

(Maximum page length should be 54 lines)

TASK 59

Recall Task 58 and amend the text as indicated. When you have completed it, proof read it carefully and print out one copy.

TASK 59

HEALTH HAZARDS CAUSED BY AUTOMATION

Apart from the traditional hazards caused by such things as badly installed electrical equipment and dangerous machinery, new hazards have appeared with office automation.

STRESS

This is now commonplace in the office, and there are many reasons for it. Boredom caused by the lack of skill needed for jobs, anxiety over adapting to computerisation, and poor environmental conditions produced by office automation are just a few of the possible causes. Even the design of buildings themselves is thought to cause stress, fatigue and other illnesses.

BACKACHE

Poorly designed seats and desks often bring about posture problems. Employers have been slow to realise that new equipment often requires new furniture, or aching muscles, headaches and backache can occur.

EYE PROBLEMS

The widespread use of VDUs has led to many complaints about eye strain and difficulty in focusing. It is important for workers to have their eyes checked before starting to use computer equipment, and to monitor the situation regularly to see if any deterioration results.

RADIATION

Though this is not thought to be a hazard, the health risks - especially to pregnant women - have not yet been determined. Many experts believe that radiation from VDUs may cause miscarriages or birth defects, but this still has to be proved.

Remove the emboldening from the side headings

Unit 7: Emboldening text

TASK 16

Key in Task 16 using double line spacing and margins of one and a half inches and one inch. Your system may insert a page break, but if not you can force a page where necessary. Remember to number the pages and to avoid leaving widows and orphans. When you have finished, proof read it carefully, then print out one copy.

TASK 16 *Set page length for 54 lines*

HOW TO SEND A FAX WITHOUT A FAX MACHINE

Although many ~~businesses~~ *firms* do have a fax machine nowadays, it is quite possible to send a fax, or to receive one, without a fax machine. All that is needed is a fax card which is slotted ~~inside~~ *into* a personal computer. ✓ This gives the advantage of being able to use the word processing facilities of the computer to edit and correct text, while offering the speed of electronic mail for sending out the information.

This means that the user can send ~~messages~~ *text* and graphics without ever committing them to paper. It is also possible to send documents containing images, signatures, company letterheads and logos. All this can be done without costing ~~an arm and a leg~~ *the earth*, and without tying the computer down to sending and receiving faxes all day long.

Installation

The fax card manufacturers all claim that installing the card is an easy matter. It is helpful to know something about the way a computer works, as the card has to be slotted in under

Continued ▶

UNIT 7 STYLE

7·1 Emboldening text

Emboldening means that the printer will overprint the same text one or more times to make it darker. This is a way of adding emphasis to those parts of a document to which you want the reader to pay special attention. The instruction to embolden is usually given when the document is keyed in. Make brief notes on how this is done, and when you are satisfied that they are correct key them into a Checklist and keep for reference.

TASK 58

Key in Task 58, emboldening the main heading and all the side headings. When you have completed it, proof read it carefully, store it on disc and print out one copy.

TASK 58

HEALTH HAZARDS IN THE OFFICE

Apart from the traditional hazards caused by such things as badly installed electrical equipment and machinery with moving parts, new hazards have appeared with office automation.

STRESS

This is now commonplace in the office, and there are many reasons for it. Boredom caused by the lack of skill needed for jobs, anxiety over adapting to computerisation, and poor environmental conditions produced by office automation are just a few of the possible causes.

BACKACHE

Poorly designed seats and desks often bring about posture problems. Employers have been slow to realise that new equipment often requires new furniture, or aching muscles, headaches and backache can occur.

EYE DISORDERS

The widespread use of VDUs has led to many complaints about eye strain and difficulty in focusing. It is important to have one's eyes checked before starting to use computer equipment, and to monitor the situation regularly to see if any deterioration results.

RADIATION

Though this is not thought to be a hazard, the health risks - especially to pregnant women - have not yet been determined.

▶ *Continued*

the cover of the machine. It may be better to find a helpful dealer who is willing to do this and ensure it is working properly, rather then try it out alone.

The card will come with its own installation program to set up the software ready for use. This means it is necessary to have a machine with a hard disc, rather than one which only uses floppy discs. A large computer memory is also essential, so nothing other than essential programs should be stored in memory.

Once the installation is over, all that remains is to follow the instructions in the user manual in order to send or receive a fax. It is helpful to understand the jargon that the manuals use, or the instructions will not be clear. Here are some commonly used terms.

Background Mode

This means that the computer can be used for other tasks while the faxes are sent out or received. It is important to purchase a fax card that operates this way and gives you the freedom to use your computer for other work.

Baud Rate

This is the transmission speed, measured in bits (binary digits) per second. For faxes, it varies between 9600 and 4800.

Continued ▶

TASK 57

This is a timed task, which should take you no longer than 40 minutes to complete and print out.

Key in Task 57 and rule up as shown. When you have completed it, proof read it carefully and print out one copy.

Please change the layout so that the category column is last. Do not use ditto marks. Rearrange the branches so they are in alphabetical order.

ROYAL CITY BANK → (Centre)

OPENING HOURS FROM JANUARY → (Centre)

BRANCH	CATEGORY	OPENING HOURS	
		WEEKDAYS	SATURDAYS
Holborn	B	9.30 – 4.30	9.00 – 12.00
Kings Cross	A	9.00 – 5.00	9.00 – 1.00
Russell Square	B	9.30 – 4.30	9.00 – 12.00
Barbican	B	9.30 – 4.30	9.00 – 12.00
Saint Pauls	C	9.30 – 3.30	10.00 – 12.00
Strand	B	9.30 – 4.30	9.00 – 12.00
Fleet Street	C	9.30 – 3.30	10.00 – 12.00
Euston	A	9.00 – 5.00	9.00 – 1.00
Covent Garden	A	9.00 – 5.00	9.00 – 1.00
Angel	C	9.30 – 3.30	10.00 – 12.00

We do not guarantee that branches will be open at the stated times, but every endeavour will be made to keep to them. For confirmation of the opening times, please ring the branch concerned.

Unit 6: Widening the page

▶ Continued

Fax Standards

The accepted standard is Group 3, though a Group 4 is being developed for colour faxes. The maximum baud rate for transmission is 9600, but the actual transmission rate depends not on the receiving device, but on the transmitting device.

File Transfer

File transfer

~~This~~ is an option which enables files to be transmitted via a fax card at a baud rate of 9600. There is no standard way of doing this, and at the moment it can only be done between computers fitted with the same type of card.

Print Out

This is a very useful feature, which enables the system to be set up so that it (automatically) prints out a fax whenever one is received. Without this feature, faxes may not actually be printed out.

Queueing

Sometimes, this is called
~~This is also known as~~ scheduling: ~~and~~ *it* makes it possible to set up a fax, but to keep it until, say, a weekend before sending it out. The purpose of this is to save on telephone connection charges.

TASK 56

Key in Task 56. When you have completed it, proof read it carefully and print out one copy.

TASK 56

J Macintosh Ltd
Woolmonger Street
EDINBURGH ED13YM

T Pinney
72 Fairway Road
EDINBURGH ED2 6RJ

STATEMENT

(centre)

(Reverse position of debit and credit columns)

DATE	REFERENCE	DEBIT	CREDIT	BALANCE
1 March	Brought Forward			300.00
2 March	Goods 194	80.30		219.70
13 March	Goods 193	5.70		214.00
16 March	Goods 195	150.00		64.00
25 March	Returns 27		30.00	94.00
31 March	Returns 28		6.00	100.00

Unit 6: Widening the page

TASK 17

This is a timed task which should take you no longer than 40 minutes to complete and print out.

Key in Task 17 using single line spacing and margins of one and a half inches and one inch. Paginate as necessary and make the amendments indicated. When you have finished, proof read it carefully, then print out one copy.

TASK 17

MENDIP MICROELECTRONICS LTD

[Number the topics in the minutes, starting with APOLOGIES]

Marketing Department

MINUTES [spaced capitals] of a meeting of the Marketing Department held at 2 pm on (insert today's date) at Head Office.

Present

Peter Lambert (Chairperson)
Neil Edwards
Janet French
Margaret Harris
John Smith
Paul Langley

[rearrange in alphabetical order, adding Michael Rutherford and Laura Winwood to the list.]

MINUTES OF LAST MEETING

These had been circulated [delete "previously"], and were approved and signed.

APOLOGIES
Apologies were received from Peter Mason.

MATTERS ARISING

There were no matters arising.

MARKET SHARE FOR MODEMS

The Chairperson distributed a document from the market research team which showed that Mendip had 15% of the modem market, though its sales were mainly through private computer retailers and the major electronic chain stores. None of the mail order retailers were stocking Mendip modems, as yet.

CHRISTMAS ADVERTISING CAMPAIGN

The Advertising Agency, Carol King Client Services, had been hired to direct a Christmas advertising campaign. This would consist of ~~a poster campaign and~~ advertisements in computer journals.

Continued ▶

TASK 55

Key in Task 55. You may change the length of the lines so that the task fits on A4 portrait paper. When you have completed it, proof read it carefully and print out one copy.

TASK 55

COUNTRY-WIDE QUESTIONNAIRE
QUEST MARKET RESEARCH

A summary of the results of our recent research into management's view of the major benefits of office automation is as follows.

[Retain the leader dots]

	All executives	Newly appointed Executives	Executives in senior positions
Facilitates decision making	75%	65%	90% 1
Raises managerial productivity	69%	70%	69% 3
Raises secretarial productivity	55%	60%	70% 2
Improves the firm's competitive stance	44%	45%	68% 4
Increases managerial accountability	30%	29%	39% 5

[Rearrange in numerical order, but do not key in the numbers]

Complete copies of the report will be available from the Office Services Department together from the end of the month with the details of the research methods used.

Unit 6: Widening the page

▶ Continued

~~COMMUNICATIONS~~ SOFTWARE LAUNCH

During the month of October, 1m copies of the newly launched communications package had been sold. The sales were mainly in London and the south-east and the product had been sold specifically as a link for Telecom Gold. The high sales had been helped by the foggy weather which had disrupted postal services.

SEPARATE BRAND NAME

Plans were confirmed to sell another package for ~~hobbyists~~ *home computer enthusiasts* under a separate brand name in the New Year. The following brand names had been suggested by the advertising agency, though agreement had not been reached.

Chatterbox

Talk Line

Connect

Global Comms

alphabetical order please

All four names were rejected by the Marketing department, and the agency would be requested to find something more appropriate

ANY OTHER BUSINESS

There was no other business.

DATE AND TIME OF NEXT MEETING

The next monthly meeting would be at 2 pm on (insert date a month from today).

Insert this item before ANY OTHER BUSINESS

SPONSORSHIP
Members of the department who were involved in the proposed sponsorship scheme were asked to present their research findings and recommendations at the next meeting.

TASK 54

Key in Task 54. You may change the length of the lines so that the task fits on A4 portrait paper. When you have completed it, proof read it carefully and print out one copy.

TASK 54   DT ELECTRONICS EQUIPMENT LEASING COSTS

Our leasing costs are shown as the weekly/equivalents rental charge, inclusive of VAT. Leasing contracts are payable on a quarterly basis or by special negotiation. Complete systems and printers with software are available on lease : please phone for details.

A wide choice of equipment by various manufacturers is available

OFFICE COMPUTERS

	WEEKLY RENTAL CHARGE EQUIVALENTS, INCLUDING VAT		
	1 YEAR CONTRACT	2 YEAR CONTRACT	5 YEAR CONTRACT
3 XT Computer	£20.00	£19.00	£17.00
2 AT Computer	£29.00	£26.00	£24.00
1 386 Computer	£44.50	£42.00	£40.00
4 Portable Computers	£35.50	£32.00	£30.50

Rearrange into numerical order, but do not key in numbers

UNIT 3: HEADERS AND FOOTERS

3.1 Using headers

A **header** is a special piece of text, such as a title, which appears at the top of every page of a document. It does not matter what the actual layout of the page is, and each page can be completely different, but the header is always the same, and is printed in the same position.

Sometimes, a header merely consists of a page number – the number on each page following in sequence, of course. This is a very useful device if a document has a large number of pages, as it saves counting the pages and renumbering them manually if the page breaks are altered. Alternatively, it could consist of several lines of text, such as a company letter heading or the title and chapter number in a book.

Before keying in Task 18, remember to make some brief notes about setting up simple headers consisting of a piece of text or a page number. When you have tested your notes in Task 18, you can key them into a Checklist and print out a copy for future reference.

TASK 18

Key in Task 18 using double line spacing and insert a page number as a header at the centre of every page, starting with page one. When you have finished, proof read it carefully, store it on disc and print out one copy.

```
TASK 18


CHANGES IN OFFICE FILING SYSTEMS

Although manual and paper-based filing systems are still used
in numerous offices throughout the country, more and more
firms are storing information electronically on computer
files.

HARD DISC FILING

Files are often stored on a hard disc, referred to as a
Winchester.  The Winchester is a magnetic disc permanently
enclosed in a dust-proof casing.  It is capable of storing
several million characters of information which can be
accessed at great speed.

FLOPPY DISC FILING

If files are not in constant use, they can be removed from the
Winchester and stored on floppy discs.  These come in various
sizes, such as 8 inches, 5.25 inches or 3.5 inches.  The last
two sizes are the most common for personal computers, and they
can store about 100 pages of A4 typescript.
```

Continued ▶

TASK 53

Recall Task 51 and widen the typing line to enable the two extra columns to be keyed in on the right of the page. It may be necessary to narrow the width between the columns so that all six will fit. When you have completed it, proof read it carefully and print out one copy on A4 paper.

Task 51 53

PC BUSINESS SOFTWARE PACKAGES ← Centre

INTEGRATED PACKAGES		DESKTOP PUBLISHING		COMMUNICATIONS	
Title	Price	Title	Price	Title	Price
Professional Office	£55.00	Vision	£499.00	Chatterbox	£185.00
Concerto	£375.00	Page Publisher	£82.00	Grape Vine	£79.00
System Integration	£49.99	Desktop Draw	£325.00	Linguist	£129.00
Planner Plus	£37.00	Paper Works	£135.00	Talk Back	£199.00
The Organiser	£230.00	The Editor	£90.00	Global Chat	£99.99
Picture Plan	£110.00	Visual Display	£69.00	Wordy	£82.00
Day by Day	£49.50	Artworks	£120.00	Recall	£90.00
Columbus	£350.00	Artscape	£215.00	Shout	£130.00
Centurian	£320.50	Domain	£450.00	ABC	£110.00
Amigo	£90.00	Purple Pages	£115.50	Listen	£95.00

Unit 6: Widening the page

▶ *Continued*

ADVANTAGES

There are major advantages in using a computer filing system, although many firms are still reluctant to give up the tried and tested paper-based system completely.

1) There is instant access to large amounts of information.

2) Distance provides no problem, as databases can be accessed in seconds through remotely based terminals.

3) Files can be constantly updated.

4) A print-out can be produced if required.

5) It is easy to move information from one file to another.

6) Tight security can be maintained so unauthorised personnel do not have access to all levels of information.

7) The saving in space is enormous.

DISADVANTAGES

1) Large computer systems are expensive to buy and maintain.

2) Staff need special training in order to use computers successfully.

3) The piles of computer print-out can produce severe storage problems.

BUSINESS PRACTICES

A large amount of business information is now electronically stored. Individual firms may keep their personnel files, customer information and financial transactions in this way. In addition, large business information enterprises are in operation which store details about companies and individuals, and sell this information for profit. For these companies, the advantages of computer filing far outweigh the disadvantages.

THE FUTURE

Although it is unlikely that paper-based filing systems will completely vanish from offices, the likelihood is that more and more filing will be done on disc. Hard disc packs for large-scale storage have been available for a considerable time, and it is unlikely that the trend towards disc storage will be reversed.

UNIT 6: TABS AND DECIMAL TABS

6.3 Widening the page

Some tables are too wide to be printed on A4 portrait paper, unless the typing line is widened to leave very small margins on either side. This can easily be done by resetting one or both margins.

You must check the pitch (number of characters per inch: see section 7.2) that is being used for printing the document, so that you can calculate the number of characters that will fit across the page.

An easy way to do this calculation is to measure the width of the paper with a ruler and multiply the number of inches of width by the pitch. This will tell you how many characters will fit across the page. Then count how many characters wide your table is, and from there you can work out where to set the margins.

As far as the margins are concerned, it is not acceptable to print documents that do not have a combined margin width of at least one inch. Wider margins are, of course, preferable.

Occasionally, work may have to be printed on A4 landscape paper, as it is just too wide to fit on portrait paper. As this may happen in the office, you should learn how to do it, if your equipment allows. However, you are not likely to be required to use landscape paper in an exam, as not all printers are wide enough to accommodate it.

The following tasks will probably require you to alter your typing line by resetting the margins. Print out your work either on A4 portrait paper or on landscape paper, if this is possible. Make notes on altering the margin settings, and when you have tested them to check that they are correct key them into a Checklist and print out a copy for future reference.

TASK 19

Key in Task 19 using double line spacing. Starting from page one, insert a header consisting of the title COMPUTERISED FILING and a page number. The title should be on the left of the page and the number on the right. When you have finished, proof read the task carefully, store it on disc and print out one copy.

TASK 19

The Filing System

Computer discs are rather like drawers of a filing cabinet. Creating document after document, with no clear idea where to store them, is the same as stuffing files into a cabinet which has no labelling on the drawers. When you have only a few files you can find them easily, but as soon as the number starts to grow, it becomes an impossible task to locate them.

To operate an efficient computerised filing system you must take the following measures.

1) You must use different discs for different types of work, just as you would use different drawers of a filing cabinet for different types of files.

2) Your documents must be put into different groups on each disc. This is like putting papers into different folders within the filing cabinet.

3) Names must be given to your discs, groups and documents. This will help you to remember what information they contain.

Using Discs

In order to keep your filing system organised, you will have to make sure you can perform several tasks on your computer. You must be able to:

format blank discs

give names to your discs, groups and documents

move documents to different groups or discs

erase unwanted documents

produce copies of documents

make back-up copies of discs.

Continued ▶

 **TASK 52**

Key in Task 52, setting decimal tabs where necessary. When you have completed it, proof read it carefully and print out one copy.

TASK 52

PRICES PER RIBBON - MINIMUM ORDER 2 RIBBONS

<u>Printer</u>	<u>Qty 2</u>	<u>Qty 5</u>	<u>Qty 10</u>	<u>Qty 100</u>
Mitsuniko LS24	£7.80	£7.50	£7.25	£3.00
Mitsuniko Colour	£12.50	£12.25	£11.50	£5.50
Sontec P6 and P222	£9.00	£8.50	£8.00	£3.75
Sontec Colour	£22.00	£21.00	£20.00	£10.00
Sukitronic LQ500/LQ850	£5.45	£5.30	£5.20	£2.50
Sukitronic Colour	£20.50	£20.00	£19.50	£9.50
Astro XB24	£6.50	£6.25	£6.00	£2.90
Astro Colour	£15.00	£14.50	£14.00	£7.00
PDS 24	£5.50	£5.00	£4.00	£3.00
PDS Special	£6.50	£6.25	£6.00	£3.00
Galaxy	£12.00	£11.50	£11.00	£7.00
Galaxy Colour	£21.00	£20.50	£19.90	£16.00
Compact	£18.50	£18.00	£17.30	£15.00
Compact Duo	£7.00	£6.70	£6.20	£4.50

▶ Continued

<u>Taking Care of Discs</u>

It is not sufficient just to know how to use your discs. You must also know how to handle them so that they are not damaged or the information they contain destroyed.

Discs are not very robust, even when they are housed in a plastic case. They can be damaged by extremes of temperature, dust, moisture or magnets. They should be stored in boxes, so that they are not crushed in any way and, of course, they should be clearly labelled. Several other precautions are necessary.

1) Never touch the magnetic surface of the disc. The sweat on your finger can do untold damage.

2) Keep the discs away from radiators, air conditioning systems and pot plants. Heat, cold and damp are likely to ruin them.

3) Do not store them near equipment which contains a magnet, such as the telephone or TV.

4) Make sure they are not in use when you remove them from your computer. The disc light should not be on, as this means information is being transferred and the disc is still in operation.

<u>A Word of Warning</u>

It is a false economy to buy cut-price discs or discs which do not carry the label of a well known manufacturer. These discs are likely to be unreliable, and not only may your information be lost, but they may even damage your machine.

TASK 51

Key in Task 51, setting decimal tabs where necessary. When you have completed it proof read it carefully and print out one copy, making sure the document has been stored for later use.

TASK 51

PC BUSINESS SOFTWARE PACKAGES

INTEGRATED PACKAGES		DESKTOP PUBLISHING	
Title	Price	Title	Price
Professional Office	£55.00	Vision	£499.00
Concerto	£375.00	Page Publisher	£82.00
System Integration	£49.99	Desktop Draw	£325.00
Planner Plus	£37.00	Paper Works	£135.00
The Organiser	£230.00	The Editor	£90.00
Picture Plan	£110.00	Visual Display	£69.00
Day by Day	£49.50	Artworks	£120.00
Columbus	£350.00	Artscape	£215.00
Centurian	£320.50	Domain	£450.00
Amigo	£90.00	Purple Pages	£115.50

Unit 6: Decimal tabs

UNIT 3
HEADERS AND FOOTERS
3.2 Using footers

A **footer** is a special piece of text which appears at the bottom of every page of a document. The footer may consist of just one line of text, or of several lines, or it may simply consist of a page number which will, of course, follow in sequence on each page. It does not matter what the actual layout of the page is, and each page can be completely different, but the footer is always the same, and is printed in the same position.

Before you start Task 20, remember to make some brief notes about setting up simple footers consisting of a piece of text or a page number. When you have tested your notes in Task 20, you can key then into a Checklist and keep them for future reference.

TASK 20

Recall Task 18 and amend it as shown. Insert a footer saying CONFIDENTIAL REPORT at the bottom of each page, in the centre. Then proof read it carefully and print out one copy.

TASK ~~18~~ 20

~~CHANGES IN~~ **NEW** OFFICE FILING SYSTEMS

Although manual and paper-based filing systems are still used in numerous offices ~~throughout the country~~, more and more firms are storing information ~~electronically~~ on computer files.

HARD DISC FILING

Files are often stored on a hard disc, ~~referred to~~ **known** as a Winchester. The Winchester is a magnetic disc permanently enclosed in a dust-proof casing. It is capable of storing several million characters of information which can be accessed at great speed.

FLOPPY DISC FILING

If files are not in constant use, they can be removed from the Winchester and stored on floppy discs. These come in various sizes, such as 8 inches, 5.25 inches or 3.5 inches. The last two sizes are the most common for personal computers, and they can store about 100 pages of A4 typescript.

Continued ▶

UNIT 6 — TABS AND DECIMAL TABS

6·2 Decimal tabs

Decimal tabs should be set when it is necessary to key in a column of figures containing decimal points. The decimal tab will align the figures to the decimal point. If there is no decimal point, the figures will be aligned to the left of the decimal tab.

Care should be taken when setting a decimal tab, as an allowance has to be made for the figures to the left of the decimal point when the tab is set. However, if the tab setting is incorrect, it is a relatively simple matter to alter it and reformat the table.

Make brief notes for your Checklist on setting decimal tabs, and when you have tested them to see that they are correct, key them in for future reference.

TASK 50

Key in Task 50, setting decimal tabs where necessary. When you have completed it, proof read it carefully and print out one copy.

TASK 50

PAYMENTS FROM PETTY CASH 2 FEBRUARY TO 8 FEBRUARY

Pack of 25 computer discs   £50.00

Spare daisy wheel   £15.99

Red carbon ribbon   £4.50

Felt tip pen   £0.26

Pack of plastic document holders   £9.00

Disinfectant for first aid kit   £0.45

'No Smoking' posters   £19.95

Self adhesive labels   £0.75
                                       _____

TOTAL   £100.90
                                       _____

▶ *Continued*

ADVANTAGES

There are major advantages in using a computer filing system, although many firms are still reluctant to give up the tried and tested paper-based system completely.

1) ~~There is instant access to large amounts of information.~~

2) Distance provides no problem, as databases can be accessed in seconds through remotely based terminals.

3) Files can be constantly updated.

4) A print-out can be produced if required. *(Alter the numbers to keep in sequence)*

5) It is easy to move information from one file to another.

6) Tight security can be maintained so unauthorised personnel do not have access to all levels of information.

7) The saving in space is enormous.

DISADVANTAGES

1) Large computer systems are expensive to buy and maintain.

2) Staff need special training in order to use computers successfully.

3) The piles of computer print-out can produce severe storage problems.

BUSINESS PRACTICE

A large amount of business information is now electronically stored. Individual firms may keep their personnel files, customer information and financial transactions in this way. In addition, large ~~business~~ information enterprises are in operation which store details about companies and individuals, and sell this information for profit. For these companies, the advantages of computer filing far outweigh the disadvantages.

THE FUTURE

Although it is unlikely that paper-based filing systems will completely vanish from offices, the likelihood is that more and more filing will be done on disc. Hard disc packs for large-scale storage have been available for a considerable time, and it is unlikely that the trend towards disc storage will be reversed.

TASK 49

Recall Task 46, and rule it up as indicated. This may require altering the layout, by moving the margins or tab settings, or changing the line spacing. The horizontal lines can probably be ruled on the word processor, but some word processing systems allow both horizontal and vertical ruling to be done. Check the instructions in your manual before you attempt to rule up. Print out one copy.

TASK 46 49

BELMONT OFFICE FURNITURE AND SUPPLIES

SEATING	REFERENCE NUMBER		DELIVERY TIME (DAYS)	
	Peat	Oatmeal	London	Elsewhere
Typist's chair	TC40	TC41	10	10-14
Executive chair	EC20	EC25	14	28
Armchair	A120	A121	28	28
Reception units	RU10	RU15	10	10-14
WP seating	WPS1	WPS2	14	21
Deluxe WP seating	DWP1	DWP2	21	28

TASK 21

Recall Task 19 and amend it as shown. Insert a footer saying INFORMATION SHEET at the bottom of each page in the centre, proof read it carefully, and print out one copy.

TASK ~~19~~ 21

The Filing System

Computer discs are rather like drawers of a filing cabinet. Creating document after document, with no clear idea where to store them, is the same as stuffing files into ~~a~~ an unlabelled cabinet ~~which has no labelling on the drawers~~. When you have only a few files you can find them easily, but as soon as the number starts to grow, it becomes an impossible task to locate them.

To operate an efficient computerised filing system you must take the following measures.

1) You must use different discs for ~~different~~ separate types of work, just as you would use different drawers of a filing cabinet for different types of files.

2) Your documents must be put into different groups on each disc. This is like putting papers into ~~different~~ separate folders within the filing cabinet.

3) Names must be given to your discs, groups and documents. This will help you to remember what information they contain.

Using Discs

In order to keep your filing system organised, you will have to make sure you can perform several tasks on your computer. You must be able to:

format blank discs

give names to your discs, groups and documents

move documents to different groups or discs

erase unwanted documents

produce copies of documents

make back-up copies of discs

} number these points

Continued ▶

Unit 3: Using footers

TASK 48

Recall Task 45, and rule it up as indicated. This may require altering the layout, by moving the margins or tab settings, or changing the line spacing. The horizontal lines can probably be ruled on the word processor, but some word processing systems allow both horizontal and vertical ruling to be done. Check the instructions in your manual before you attempt to rule up. Print out one copy.

TASK 45̶ 48

COMPUTER PURCHASES

Mercury Computers			
Type	Monitor	Disc	Speed
PC30	12" mono display	Single drive	8 MHz
PC30	14" colour display	Twin drive hard disc	8 MHz
PC40	14" colour display	Twin drive	12 MHz
PC50	14" colour display	Single drive hard disc	20 MHz
Zen Computers			
Type	Monitor	Disc	Speed
M200	12" colour display	20 MB hard disc	10 MHz
M250	12" colour display	40 MB hard disc	20 MHz

Unit 6: Setting text in columns

▶ Continued

<u>Taking Care of Discs</u>

~~It is not sufficient just to know how to use your discs. You must also know how to handle them so that they are not damaged or the information they contain destroyed.~~

Discs are not very robust, even when they are housed in a plastic case. They can be damaged by extremes of temperature, dust, moisture or magnets. They should be stored in boxes, so that they are not crushed in any way and, of course, they should be clearly labelled. Several other precautions are necessary.

1) Never touch the magnetic surface of the disc. The sweat on your finger can do untold damage.

2) Keep the discs away from radiators, ~~air conditioning systems~~ **draughty windows** and pot plants. Heat, cold and damp are likely to ruin them.

3) Do not store them near equipment which contains a magnet, such as the telephone or TV. **This will destroy the information they contain.**

4) Make sure they are not in use when you remove them from your computer. The disc light should not be on, as this means information is being transferred and the disc is still in operation.

<u>A Word of Warning</u>

It is a false economy to buy ~~cut-price~~ **cheap** discs or discs which do not carry the label of a well-known manufacturer. These discs are likely to be ~~unreliable~~ **(counterfeits)**, and not only may your information be lost, but they may even damage your machine.

TASK 47

Recall Task 44 and rule it up as indicated. This may require altering the layout, by moving the margins or tab settings, or changing the line spacing. The horizontal lines can probably be ruled on the word processor, but some word processing systems allow both horizontal and vertical ruling to be done. Check the instructions in your manual before you attempt to rule up. Print out one copy.

TASK ~~44~~ 47

EQUIPMENT FAULTS REPORTED IN JUNE		
<u>Equipment</u>	<u>Location</u>	<u>Description of Fault</u>
Audio machine	Sales department	Destroys tapes
Word processor	Workstation 6	Faulty disc drive
Dot matrix printer	Computer section	Paper feed jammed
Fax machine	Mail room	Will not operate
Photocopier	Reception area	Collator not working

Unit 6: Setting text in columns

TASK 22

Key in Task 22, incorporating the amendments. Insert a header saying SECOND DRAFT, and a footer consisting of a page number. Both header and footer should be centred, and should start on the first page. When you have completed it, proof read it carefully and print out one copy in double line spacing.

TASK 22

MEMORANDUM

TO All workstation users   REF PH/CB
FROM Computer Centre Manager   DATE (insert today's date)

BACK-UP PROCEDURES

It has been brought to my attention recently that we have had a series of disasters because a rather haphazard system of backing up files has been in force.

I cannot stress more strongly how necessary it is to safeguard your software, and I am sure you will all agree with me that it is even more important than safeguarding hardware. If your own files or the program files are destroyed it may not be possible to re-create them within a reasonable period of time. However, any hardware that is damaged or destroyed can be replaced very quickly. The message is clear, YOU MUST BACK UP YOUR FILES.

It is not a safe policy to leave files stored on the hard disc overnight, because if there are problems with the computer system or if there is a sudden power cut, it may not be possible to retrieve them. The following procedure should, therefore, be adopted.

(Leave 20 clear lines here for a diagram)

Continued ▶

TASK 46

Key in Task 46, setting simple tabs where required. When you have completed it, proof read it carefully and print out one copy, making sure the document has been stored for later use.

TASK 46

BELMONT OFFICE FURNITURE AND SUPPLIES

SEATING	REFERENCE NUMBER		DELIVERY TIME (DAYS)	
	Peat	Oatmeal	London	Elsewhere
Typist's chair	TC40	TC41	10	10-14
Executive chair	EC20	EC25	14	28
Armchair	A120	A121	28	28
Reception units	RU10	RU15	10	10-14
WP seating	WPS1	WPS2	14	21
Deluxe WP seating	DWP1	DWP2	21	28

Unit 6: Setting text in columns

▶ Continued

1) At the end of each working day, all work should be filed from the hard disc on to a labelled floppy disc.

2) Two sets of back-up discs, A and B, should be created for storing the day's work.

3) After each day's processing, the work should be stored alternately on A or B.

This system means that if the current discs are destroyed, there will always be a current back-up copy. Even if this is also destroyed, the remaining back-up copy will contain the previous day's processing.

At one time or another, we have all suffered the terrible experience of losing work because no back-up has been available. This has meant that several days' or even weeks' hard labour has gone down the drain. Hopefully, the new system will prevent this ever happening again.

TASK 45

Key in Task 45, setting simple tabs where required. When you have completed it, proof read it carefully and print out one copy, making sure the document has been stored for later use.

TASK 45

COMPUTER PURCHASES

Mercury Computers

Type	Monitor	Disc	Speed
PC 30	12" Mono display	Single drive	8 MHz
PC 30	14" Colour display	Twin drive hard disc	8 MHz
PC 40	14" Colour display	Twin drive	12 MHz
PC 50	14" Colour display	Single drive hard disc	20 MHz

Zen Computers

Type	Monitor	Disc	Speed
M200	12" Colour display	20 MB hard disc	10 MHz
M250	12" Colour display	40 MB hard disc	20 MHz

UNIT 3 — HEADERS AND FOOTERS

3.3 Selective headers and footers

Often, there will be occasions when you do not want the same header and footer to appear on every page. If, for example, the header is a page number, you will probably not want to number the very first page of your document, especially if it is the title page.

Similarly, you may want to put a footer at the bottom of most pages, except perhaps for one of them. For example, you may want the word 'continued' to appear as a footer on all pages except the final page of your document.

Before keying in Task 23, remember to make some brief notes about setting up selective headers — especially those that consist of a page number. You can use Task 23 to test whether your notes on selective headers are correct.

Then make notes on setting up selective footers and test these on Task 23. Finally, if you are happy that your notes are adequate, key them into a Checklist and print out a copy.

TASK 23

Key in Task 23 using double line spacing. Insert a header consisting of a page number to start from the second page of the document. The page numbers should be in the centre of each page. When you have finished, proof read the task carefully, store it on disc and print out one copy.

```
TASK 23


                          MEMORANDUM

TO    All Departmental Managers        REF AJ/KM

FROM   Computer Centre Manager         DATE (Insert today's date)

THE DATA PROTECTION ACT 1984

After talks with our legal advisers, I am circulating this
memo in an attempt to clarify some of the points which concern
the use of data in our organisation.

I hope it will set your minds at rest that it is only
'personal data' which is covered by the Act, so it is not
necessary to reveal our trading secrets to our competitors!

The widespread use of computers today has led to the passing
of this  piece of legislation,   which regulates 'personal
data' (information about people) and 'data users' (the people
or organisations who collect and use the information).
```

Continued

UNIT 6: TABS AND DECIMAL TABS

6·1 Setting text in columns

Tab settings are used to display text or figures in columns. This means that it is possible to key in the work quickly and easily, as the cursor will jump from column to column when the tab key on the keyboard is pressed.

If alterations are required or errors have been made in setting out the columns, it is a simple matter to change the layout and reformat the work before printing out.

Most word processing systems have both a simple tab and a decimal tab. Some may also have more advanced tab settings, such as a tab which will justify text on the right, or one which will centre text. These you can investigate by yourself later.

First, make notes on setting a simple tab and test them by keying in Task 44. If you are happy with your notes, key them into a Checklist and print out a copy for future reference.

TASK 44

Key in Task 44, setting simple tabs where required. When you have completed it, proof read it carefully and print out one copy, making sure the document has been stored for later use.

TASK 44

EQUIPMENT FAULTS REPORTED IN JUNE

Equipment	Location	Description of Fault
Audio machine	Sales department	Destroys tapes
Word processor	Workstation 6	Faulty disc drive
Dot matrix printer	Computer section	Paper feed jammed
Fax machine	Mail room	Will not operate
Photocopier	Reception area	Collator not working

▶ *Continued*

It has also been passed to ensure that data can move freely between the United Kingdom and other European countries with similar laws, so that international trade is maintained.

WHAT INFORMATION IS COVERED?

The Act only covers information processed by a computer. Traditional paper files kept in filing cabinets or other storage systems are not covered.

Only information relating to individual people is within the scope of the Act, so it does not deal with information about companies and their trading partners.

WHAT IS PERSONAL DATA?

This term refers to information about people who are alive today and can be identified as individuals from the data which has been kept about them.

This does not mean that the data has to contain a person's name. It may consist of a pay roll number or an employee number, but if an individual can actually be identified from the data, it can be classified as 'personal data', and will be covered by the Act.

WHO ARE DATA USERS?

These are people or organisations that collect and control personal data in the form of computer files. However, this does not mean that the data user must own a computer. It is possible for a firm to use a computer bureau to handle its data requirements. A data user is, therefore, a person or organisation which decides what information is collected, and how it is used.

Recall Task 23 and insert the word CONTINUED as a footer at the right-hand margin of all the pages, except for the last one. Retain the original headers consisting of page numbers. Print out one copy in double line spacing.

▶ *Continued*

This is a timed task which should take you no longer than 15 minutes to complete and print out.

Key in Task 43, recalling the relevant phrases and inserting them at the points marked. Remember to key in today's date and carry out any corrections required. Proof read it carefully and print out one copy. There is no need to copy this letter, as only one print-out is required.

TASK 43

Global Travel Service Ltd
Unit 21
Weston Favell Shopping Centre
BRISTOL
BR4 9TL

Dear Mr Metcalfe

INSTALLATION OF (Insert phrase 1)

Further to our recent ~~visit~~ *conversation* (stet), we confirm that our contractors (Insert phrase 4) will be starting work on the installation next Monday.

We estimate that the work will take (Insert phrase 5) to complete, and the electricity supply will need to be disconnected for a maximum of (Insert phrase 7)

In addition, completion of the work will require the use of (Insert phrase 8), but we shall endeavour to keep any disruption to a minimum. [new paragraph] Protective coverings will also be supplied for your computers, fittings and furnishings to prevent damage from dirt and dust. However, we would advise you to warn your staff about the forthcoming disruption and the hazards caused by the drilling.

Yours sincerely

(Insert phrase 9)

TASK 24

This is a timed task which should take you no longer than 40 minutes to complete and print out.

Key in Task 24 using double line spacing. Insert a header consisting of a page number to start from the second page of the document. The page numbers should be in the centre of each page. Insert the word CONTINUED as a footer at the right-hand margin of all the pages, except for the last one. When you have finished, proof read the task carefully and print out one copy.

TASK 24

THE DATA PROTECTION ACT AND YOU

REPORT

If personal details about you is kept by a firm or by a computer bureau, the law gives you certain rights concerning this information.

ACCESS

Obviously, it is impossible to judge whether the information is correct or not if you do not know what information is being kept, so the law gives you the right of access to the information kept about yourself.

To gain access to it, you must make a written request, asking to be supplied with a copy of any information that is being kept about you.

It is quite lawful to charge a fee for supplying this information, as printing and postage charges may be incurred, and searching through computer records to provide the information may be quite time-consuming.

Continued ▶

TASK 43

Key in and store the following phrases for use in Task 43, which will be a timed task.

Phrase 1	COMMUNICATIONS EQUIPMENT
Phrase 2	SATELLITE DISH
Phrase 3	Multilink Ltd
Phrase 4	Satcom International
Phrase 5	approximately 5 working days
Phrase 6	1 hour
Phrase 7	30 minutes
Phrase 8	drilling equipment
Phrase 9	Gillian Lewis Contracts Manager
Phrase 10	Martin Ford Engineering Manager

Continued ▶

▶ Continued

ALTERATION AND COMPENSATION

Once you have obtained ~~the~~ whatever information is kept about you and studied it, you must judge whether it is accurate or not. Misleading information can be corrected by applying to the County Courts. However, it must be shown clearly that the information is inaccurate.

An opinion is not a statement of fact, so it does not constitute an inaccuracy even if it shows you in an unfavourable light.

Compensation may be given for ~~certain~~ various reasons. ✓ If you suffer financial loss or personal injury because of the inaccuracy of the information, compensation may be payable. This is provided the organisation responsible for the data cannot prove that reasonable care was taken to obtain the information.

Compensation can also be paid if information was lost or an unauthorised disclosure was made, and as a result you suffered some sort of damage. // Damage does not refer to mental distress, but means financial loss or physical injury. No compensation will be awarded if the personal information does not have to be registered by law, but is kept purely by choice.

> If reasonable care was taken, you will get nothing.

Continued ▶

▶ Continued

Now key in Task 42, recalling the relevant phrases and inserting them at the points marked. Address the document to 'all personal secretaries', and remember to key in today's date and carry out any corrections required. Proof read it carefully and print out one copy. There is no need to copy this document, as only one print-out is required.

TASK 42

(Insert phrase 1)

COMPUTERISED TELEPHONE SYSTEM

It has been brought to my attention that many of (Insert phrase 3) are unaware of how to operate the new computerised system correctly. I would point out that it is no longer possible to make long distance calls without contacting the switchboard. For important customers outside the local area, a code has been developed so that they can be contacted directly.

Accordingly, I have arranged a (Insert phrase 6) with a representative from British Telecom to try and ensure correct usage in future.

May I remind you all how important it is to answer the phone promptly when it rings and to announce your own identity and that of the firm. Many potential customers are lost if they hear a surly voice at the end of the line, so it is essential to cultivate a pleasant speaking voice and a polite tone.

Kindly forward to me your department and name, (Insert phrase 8) I will circulate (Insert phrase 10)   in the near future. In the meantime, I suggest you seek guidance from (Insert phrase 2) if you encounter difficulties. An instruction manual for the new system is being printed, and I hope to be able to distribute it to you all, together with the new list of staff and their extension numbers, by the end of the week.

Separate training arrangements have been made for (Insert phrase 5)   and they will receive further information about these shortly.

Unit 5: Inserting stored text in a standard document

▶ Continued

MAKING COMPLAINTS

You do have the right to complain to the Registrar if you consider that you have suffered an injustice. This does not mean you have to take the matter to the County Courts. Going to Court is an expensive procedure, and it is unnecessary unless damages are being sought and compensation is expected.

The Registrar is obliged to investigate all complaints. He must ~~give a ruling~~ pass judgement on a complaint, and must justify his decision by explaining the reasons for it. He will try and seek a solution which is acceptable to both parties concerned [once the decision has been made].

Guidance may also be offered to organisations using data if they are not sure how the Act operates. In extreme cases the Registrar may bring prosecutions if he thinks the Act is clearly being ~~ignored~~ flouted.

Although privacy is extremely important, it is necessary to reveal the identity of the person complaining in order to investigate a complaint thoroughly. // If the matter has to go to Court, publicity may be incurred, though the Registrar will do his best to ensure maximum privacy. If you do make a complaint, you will have to accept that publicity may be the consequence [regardless of whether or not you win your case].

TASK 42

Key in and store the following phrases for use in Task 42.

Phrase 1	MEMORANDUM
	FROM Barry Stephens
	Personnel Manager
	TO DATE
Phrase 2	the receptionist/telephonist staff
Phrase 3	the secretarial staff
Phrase 4	the clerical team
Phrase 5	the management team
Phrase 6	half-day training course
Phrase 7	full-day training course
Phrase 8	if you are interested in attending the course
Phrase 9	if you are not interested in attending the course
Phrase 10	details of the arrangements for this course

Continued ▶

Unit 5: Inserting stored text in a standard document

UNIT 4 DEALING WITH PARAGRAPHS

4·1 Inserting fresh information

This unit deals with making large-scale changes to documents, such as inserting new paragraphs, duplicating text within a document and moving sections of text from one place in a document to another. Exam papers usually include examples of such drastic changes to help prepare you for the sort of large-scale alterations you may have to deal with once you start work.

To make things easier, the unit has been divided into three sections, each dealing with one sort of major alteration, and each revising common correction signs which are used in exams and in businesses.

The first of these – inserting fresh information – you have probably dealt with before on a small scale. Check your instructions for inserting text, and make sure that they also apply to inserting large portions of text. Make notes on the procedure used by your word processing system for inserting large portions of new text, and when you have tested them to see if they are correct, key them into a Checklist for future reference.

TASK 25

Key in Task 25, making alterations as shown and numbering the second and any subsequent pages. When you have finished, proof read it carefully, then store it on disc and print out one copy.

TASK 25

FIRST IMPRESSIONS COUNT ← (centre)

Many firms do not pay ~~sufficient~~ *enough* attention to receiving ✓ visitors. Customers, clients and callers soon get irritated if their arrival goes unnoticed, or if the receptionist ~~carries on~~ *continues* chatting and pays no attention to them. It is, therefore, most important to have a receptionist who is alert and aware of her responsibilities and deals with visitors ~~in an efficient manner~~. (efficiently)

However, it is not just the receptionist who can create a ~~good~~ *favourable* impression of the firm. If the reception area itself is not clean, tidy and well designed, the visitor can get ~~an adverse impression~~. Everyone is quick to notice overflowing ashtrays, drooping pot plants or magazines and newspapers which are torn and dog-eared. A general air of neglect makes the visitor think that the firm is not ~~doing well~~. ~~prospering~~. ✓ (the wrong idea)

Continued ▶

TASK 41

Recall your copy of the letter in Task 40. Then recall the relevant phrases, inserting them at the points marked. Proof read it carefully and print out one copy.

TASK ~~2~~ 41

Ref GE/(your initials)

(Insert today's date)

Dear Property Owner

(Insert phrase 2)

We have many companies on our books who are urgently looking for *(Insert Phrase 4)* in your area. Our clients realise that location and accessibility are key elements for a sound investment in commercial property. Many are seeking properties for purchase, and are willing to make a quick exchange should suitable accommodation become vacant. We do, however, have many clients who are interested in short or long term rentals and are prepared to effect a deal without delay.

Most of these companies have already *(Insert phrase 5)* and, in addition, some are being sponsored by government initiatives. We also have our own independent financial adviser who can put prospective purchasers in touch with a range of financial institutions committed to offering their support in this developing area.

If any of your leaseholders are *(Insert phrase 7)* we should be happy to *(Insert phrase 10)* and we look forward to hearing from you on this matter in the near future.

Even if this is not the case, you may perhaps care to call in at our offices and inspect the plans of several imposing developments in the vicinity. These units will shortly be offered for investment or occupation on a low start finance scheme. We should be happy to discuss the arrangements with you at any time.

Yours sincerely
GOODMAN ESTATES

Unit 5: Inserting stored text in a standard document

▶ Continued

<u>Furniture</u>

Comfortable seating must be installed in the reception area, a coffee table for setting down refreshments, and a coat rack. It is as well to make provision for wet weather by also providing an umbrella stand with a drip pan.

(Insert paragraph A here)

<u>Decor</u>

~~Psychologists claim that reds and yellows create an aggressive atmosphere, while a calming air is provided by the colours blue and green. Whether this is true or not, it is not wise to use a colouring scheme that is too strident or extreme, as apart from the image it creates, it can soon become dated and need replacing.~~ What is most important is the creation of a warm, pleasant atmosphere with sufficient light for reading. Callers do not want to feel that their visit will be a harrowing experience. This is the effect poor decor can produce.

(Insert paragraph B here)

<u>Magazines and Newspapers</u>

All organisations like to show they are aware of ~~what is happening in the world~~ world events, so it is common practice to subscribe to ~~a~~ quality newspapers for visitors to read.

In addition, many firms provide trade journals in the reception area, together with copies of the latest company newsletter and a display of their most recent products. Obviously, when these become ~~out-of-date~~ obsolete ✓, they must be discarded and replaced.

<u>Refreshments</u>

It usual to provide the visitor with a hot drink on arrival, especially if some delay has occurred or is anticipated (before the start of the meeting). Office reception areas are usually equipped with tea and coffee making equipment or provide a vending machine to set the visitor at ease.

Paragraph A

Nothing looks so bad as a reception area with dilapidated furniture and a stained carpet, so care must be taken to provide durable seating and stain-resistant flooring.

Paragraph B

<u>Indoor plants</u>

A visually pleasing environment can be created by the use of pot plants and flowers. They ~~can~~ add natural colour to the decor and their flowing lines soften the angular shape of the office fittings.

▶ Continued

Now key in Task 40 and make a copy for later use. Recall the relevant phrases and insert them at the points marked. Proof read it carefully and print out one copy.

```
TASK 40

Ref GE/(your initials)

(Insert today's date)



Dear Property Owner
     (Insert phrase 1)

We have many companies on our books who are urgently looking
for      (Insert phrase 3)         in your area.  Our clients
realise that location and accessibility are key elements for a
sound investment in commercial property.  Many are seeking
properties for purchase, and are willing to make a quick
exchange should suitable accommodation become vacant.  We do,
however, have many clients who are interested in short or long
term rentals and are prepared to effect a deal without delay.

Most of these companies have already (Insert phrase 6)
and, in addition, some are being sponsored by government
initiatives.  We also have our own independent financial
adviser who can put prospective purchasers in touch with a
range of financial institutions committed to offering their
support in this developing area.

If any of your leaseholders are (Insert phrase 8)
we should be happy to  (Insert phrase 9)        and we look
forward to hearing from you on this matter in the near future.

Even if this is not the case, you may perhaps care to call in
at our offices and inspect the plans of several imposing
developments in the vicinity.  These units will shortly be
offered for investment or occupation on a low start finance
scheme.  We should be happy to discuss the arrangements with
you at any time.

Yours sincerely
GOODMAN ESTATES
```

TASK 26

Key in Task 26, making alterations as shown and numbering the second and any subsequent pages. When you have finished, proof read it carefully, then store it on disc and print out one copy.

TASK 26

VISITORS TO THE OFFICE — *centre*

Companies often have strict rules about receiving visitors, in order to prevent industrial espionage and theft and to ensure that Strangers do not wander around the building unattended. // Visitors are usually asked to sign the Visitors' Book or Reception Register on arrival, and may then be given some form of identification, such as a badge or pass. Secretaries are usually telephoned from the reception area so that the visitor can be escorted to the manager's office, provided a prior appointment has been made.

The Appointments Diary

Visitors can seldom be received without an appointment, but not all managers are willing to devote large periods of time to talking to salesmen or representatives. Often they prefer to restrict the amount of time given to each visitor. It is prudent to discuss with each manager the preferred practice. Common sense also plays a part in making a sensible system, and here are some points to bear in mind.

(Insert A as paragraph 1 and adjust the numbering)

1   Do not make appointments too close to lunchtimes or in the late afternoons in case they run over. *This can be most inconvenient.*

2   Keep appointments reasonably short so that they do not seem excessively time-consuming if they take longer.

3   Never book a manager with appointments all day long. He or she has other commitments each day, and cannot spend the whole time talking to visitors.

4   Before the appointment takes place, give the manager the relevant documents to peruse so that he or she knows what the meeting will be about.

5   Clearly note down in the appointments register the visitor's name, designation and organisation with a brief statement giving the reason for the visit, so that there is no misunderstanding when the visitor arrives.

Continued ▶

TASK 40

Key in and store the following phrases for use in Tasks 40 and 41.

Phrase 1	BLACKTHORN INDUSTRIAL ESTATE
Phrase 2	WESTBURY TOWN CENTRE
Phrase 3	office accommodation
Phrase 4	retail premises
Phrase 5	reached the end of their present lease
Phrase 6	arranged suitable finance
Phrase 7	reaching the end of their term
Phrase 8	interested in subletting
Phrase 9	discuss a suitable arrangement with you
Phrase 10	re-let the property

Continued ▶

Unit 5: Inserting stored text in a standard document

▶ Continued

6   *Sometimes, of course* Be prepared to rescue a manager from appointments which are clearly overrunning by providing a plausible excuse. ~~unless~~ it is clear that the appointment is intended to continue.

(Insert B as paragraph 8 and adjust the numbering)

7   If there is too much pressure for appointments, enquire whether other members of the department can receive visitors ~~instead of the manager~~. Very often, section heads ~~can~~ *will* relieve the pressure by receiving some of the firm's visitors.

8   When a ~~visitor~~ *caller* arrives without an appointment, do not ✓ confirm that the manager is in the office without first finding out if he or she wants to see the visitor or not.

Useful Information Sources

The receptionist would be well advised to keep some helpful information sources to hand. An essential item is the current version of the company's internal telephone directory giving the names, designations, locations and extension numbers of the firm's personnel. A telephone message pad or notebook for taking down messages and making a log of visitors to the firm is also indispensable.

Other useful items are a set of telephone and fax directories, a streetfinder and British Rail timetables. Duplicate maps of the firm's premises and the locality would also be helpful to guide visitors.

For emergencies, it would also be wise to have a list of managers' and security officers' home telephone numbers, the company doctor or nurse and a first aid kit and illustrated manual.

A
Before making an appointment, make sure that there are no other events that day or week which would mean that the manager is unable to devote sufficient time to it.

B
Make sure that the visitor is offered tea or coffee either before or during the appointment, in accordance with the firm's established practice.

TASK 39

Recall your copy of the letter in Task 38. Then recall the relevant phrases and insert them at the points marked. Proof read it carefully and print out one copy.

```
TASK 39

Ref MS/(your initials)

(Insert today's date)

(Insert phrase 2)

We are writing to tell you that our (Insert phrase 4)   is
about to open and to invite you to the launch which will take
place at  (Insert phrase 5)          on Saturday 3 May.

Many items will be sold at a large discount, but we are sure
that you will be particularly interested in the following:

personal computers

portable computers and hand helds

(Insert phrase 7)

computer games

(Insert phrase 9)

general accessories

There are many other bargains in store and we offer
substantial trade and bulk discounts.  We look forward to
seeing you on the opening day.

(Insert phrase 10)
```

Unit 5: Inserting stored text in a standard document

UNIT 4 — DEALING WITH PARAGRAPHS

4.2 Copying text within a document

Sometimes, a section of text is duplicated within a document, and to save keying it in a second time most word processing systems offer a facility for copying text.

Some systems simply call this facility 'Copy Text'. Others use another term, such as 'Copy and Paste'. What usually happens is that the portion of the original text to be copied is highlighted, then stored temporarily so that it can be recalled later on in the document. It may even be possible to repeat the text several times in the same document by using this facility.

First of all, make brief notes on how your system operates this facility and use them to complete Task 27. When you can confirm that they are correct, key them into a Checklist and print out a copy for future reference.

TASK 27

Key in Task 27, making alterations as shown and numbering the second and any subsequent pages. When you have finished, proof read it carefully, then store it on disc and print out one copy.

TASK 27

MEMORANDUM (Spaced capitals)

TO   All ~~Personal~~ WP Secretaries   REF   JS/MC

FROM Office Services Manager   DATE   (Insert today's date)

The computer section have now produced their report on the use of electronic 'information managers', which we are hoping to install in the New Year. For those of you who are not acquainted with this term, an 'information manager' is a software package which provides a computer-based diary, address book and notepad. Apart from making and viewing entries, it enables you to make lists, calculate expenses, write letters and manage your time more efficiently.

I am giving a brief explanation below on the use of the diary and address book facilities, and will be arranging a demonstration and question-and-answer session in the near future.

[Training sessions will, of course, take place as soon as the software is purchased.] (Copy to △)

WHAT IS AN ELECTRONIC DIARY? An electronic diary is a software package which replaces the traditional book-bound method of regulating the way diaries and appointments are kept. The packages available are integrated and link various familiar features.
※ (Copy paragraph to here)

Continued ▶

▶ Continued

Now key in Task 38 and make a copy for use later. Recall the relevant phrases and insert them at the points marked. Proof read it carefully and print out one copy.

```
TASK 38

Ref MS/(your initials)

(Insert today's date)

(Insert phrase 1)

We are writing to tell you that our (Insert phrase 3)   is
about to open and to invite you to the launch which will take
place at (Insert phrase 6)         on Saturday 3 May.
Many items will be sold at a large discount, but we are sure
that you will be particularly interested in the following:

personal computers

portable computers and hand helds
(Insert phrase 8)
computer games
(Insert phrase 9)
general accessories

There are many other bargains in store and we offer
substantial trade and bulk discounts.  We look forward to
seeing you on the opening day.

(Insert phrase 10)
```

▶ *Continued*

1. word processing and electronic notepad
2. spreadsheet and database
3. communications
4. calculator and five-year calendar reference tables

FEATURES OF THE ELECTRONIC DIARY [These features are all subject to the use of a security password agreed within the organisation.] (copy to ✱)

1. The actual diary and appointments facility allows a five-year calendar and rolling diary to be scanned. Entries can be made using the word processing facility.

2. Diary pages can be ~~scanned~~ *viewed* either slowly or quickly, and the day is divided into morning, afternoon and evening. It is also possible to ~~scan~~ *view* by week, month or year.

3. Appointments and reminders can be entered at any time *or place* and for any duration. Periods can be 'booked' or removed to indicate that no interruption should be made to work.

Reminders can be inserted and jobs for the day can be prioritised – even well in advance of the day concerned! A link with the electronic notepad can allow more lengthy messages to be accessed to serve as memory joggers.

4. A link with a local area network ~~can mean~~ *means* that the diaries of personnel within the building can be searched, and arrangements made and entered for meetings at a mutually convenient time and date. It is also possible to order transport, equipment or accommodation from a central office services area.

5. Other packages can also be used and incorporated in the diary. Word processing is the most commonly used of these packages.

Ⓐ (copy paragraph to here)

THE ADDRESS BOOK The address book is arranged in alphabetical order and will probably be displayed on screen like open pages of a traditional address book. After selecting the correct letter of the alphabet, you can then key in a person's name, company address, phone and fax numbers.

You will be able to use the address book to do other tasks, such as making lists of all the people connected with a particular firm, or all the firms selling a certain product. This is done by using the database facility and making a mini database for each category you want to list.

The electronic notepad is useful here, as you can key in additional information about the categories you have created. You can also set up letter templates and automatically insert details, such as name, address and date, from either the address book or the database. // You can even keep track of expenses, such as telephone calls or faxes, by using the integrated calculator.

UNIT 5

INSERTING STORED TEXT
5·3 Inserting stored text in a standard document

Stored text is not always used to create completely new documents. Sometimes stored phrases can be inserted in an existing document. This is often the case in legal work, where a library of standard clauses is often created so that they can be used over and over again.

The following tasks give more practice in storing phrases and retrieving them for incorporation in standard documents. It will be necessary to copy the standard document, so that it can be used more than once, and you will have to make sure you know how to do this. Refer to your manual or the 'Copy Text' instructions from Unit 4. When you are sure your notes are correct, key them into a Checklist and keep for reference.

TASK 38

Key in the following phrases and store for use in Tasks 38 and 39.

```
Phrase 1      Dear Customer

Phrase 2      Dear Sir/Madam

Phrase 3      Annual Sale and Discount Period

Phrase 4      new store

Phrase 5      Sunrise Computers, Grosvenor Shopping Precinct

Phrase 6      Sunrise Computers, Arndale Centre

Phrase 7      computer peripherals and components

Phrase 8      standard business software

Phrase 9      printers and plotters

Phrase 10     Yours truly


              Michael Spencer
              Store Manager
```

Continued ▶

TASK 28

Key in Task 28, making alterations as shown and numbering the second and any subsequent pages. When you have finished, proof read it carefully, then print out one copy.

TASK 28

[NEW PRODUCT FEATURE - RING 071 212 2122 FOR MORE DETAILS]

<u>Organising The Boss</u>

Business people ~~Managers~~ no longer have to rely on the receptionist and personal secretary to keep them organised. An Organiser is a pocket computer about the size of a hand-held calculator which can be used by executives on the move as a notebook or Filofax. It can also be used as a data gathering device, and it has proved to be so useful that more than 300,000 are sold **each** ~~per~~ year.

Ⓐ (Copy paragraph to here)

As it has its own tiny keypad, it can be used both as a word processor and as a calculator and offers the same power as a much larger computer. It was designed primarily as a personal time management system but is now being used by large corporations as a remote terminal for their centralised computer systems.

Rather than being used just as a database of addresses and phone numbers and as an electronic diary to help a manager keep appointments, an Organiser has many other uses. **Some examples are as follows.**

* They are used by shops in conjunction with bar code readers as an inventory control system.

* Telephone engineers record details of repair jobs and travelling time on them instead of on manual work sheet**s**.

* Insurance Companies and Finance Brokers have replaced their traditional 'rate books' with them so that clients can be given a complex quotation on the spot.

* ~~Club Secretaries use them for updating membership and subscriptions records.~~

* Factories use them for stock-taking, as do department stores and large offices.

For the office manager who does not have these specialised uses for them, they are a powerful calculator, a notepad and a diary and appointments register. In addition, they can store all sorts of useful information like the international dialling codes and local times for hundreds of cities and countries throughout the world.

* **Estate Agents use them to jot down details of properties they view.**

Continued ▶

TASK 37

Using the standard paragraphs stored on disc in Task 36, send letters to the job applicants listed in Task 37. Use the paragraphs and infill data indicated. When you have finished, proof read the letters carefully and print out.

TASK 37

1) Paragraph 1 — Infill: Ref MW/your initials
   Today's date
   Mrs Margaret Owen
   39 Coppice Drive
   SURBITON KT1 9SD
   Dear Mrs Owen
   word processor operator

   Paragraph 2 — Infill: the 'Surbiton Times'

   Paragraph 4

2) Paragraph 1 — Infill: Ref MW/your initials
   Today's date
   Mr Andrew Reed
   7 Manor Court
   Lockwood Road
   SURBITON KT2 4SB
   Dear Mr Reed
   technical editor

   Paragraph 3 — Infill: 5 February
   2 pm

   Paragraph 4

3) Paragraph 1 — Infill: Ref MW/your initials
   Today's date
   Mrs Joanne Lavery
   2 Windsor Road
   RICHMOND RN1 9HM
   Dear Mrs Lavery
   technical editor

   Paragraph 3 — Infill: 6 February
   10 am

   Paragraph 4

Unit 5: Using stored phrases to create a document

▶ *Continued*

<u>The Portable Office</u>

Obviously, all the information stored on an Organiser can be downloaded onto a desktop computer, if required, so that it can be edited, stored or used to update an existing database.

An Organiser can be treated like a portable office, as it is possible to use it for so many tasks. Anyone with a computer at home can print out information from the Organiser at the end of the day. If this is not necessary, the information can just be stored, or it can be transmitted to company headquarters if required.

People whose work keeps them frequently on the move find them an especial blessing. They do not even have to call in at the office at the end of the day, as their work has been safely stored by the Organiser. They can either deal with it at home, if they have a desktop computer, or leave it until they next visit the office - which may not be for some time.

~~The Organiser's appearing on the market are becoming more and more sophisticated and offering larger displays and built-in features. There are also some fascinating peripherals on offer, such as a portable dot-matrix thermal printer, a magnetic card reader and a barcode reader especially designed for retailers.~~

[The Organiser, which started life as an electronic notepad/diary for the busy executive, is now a highly versatile machine with an abundance of special program packs which can be slotted into the back.] *(Copy to Ⓐ)*

To name but a few, these include:

*   Spell Checker

*   Finance Pack   ← *(* Mini Database)*

*   Pocket Spreadsheet

*   Portfolio Management   ← *(* Travel Pack)*

*   Communications Link.

No-one can fault the Organiser for its size or weight. It is so small it can easily be slipped into a jacket pocket. For this reason, it is often used for non-business purposes. Organisers are very addictive! People all over the country are throwing away their diaries, notebooks and Filofaxes, and slipping an Organiser into briefcases and shopping bags. The probability is that you will soon be doing the same.

 Ⓐ *(Copy paragraph to here)*

TASK 36

Key in the paragraphs in Task 36 and store for later use. Insert a symbol, as shown, at points where specific information will have to be inserted. Be sure you make a note of the reference under which you have stored each paragraph, as they will be required in Task 37.

```
TASK 36


PARAGRAPH 1

Ref MW/@

@

@

Dear @

Thank you for your application for the post of @ which was
recently advertised.


PARAGRAPH 2

There was a very large response to the advertisement in @, and
we regret to tell you that your application has not been
successful.  However, let me take this opportunity of thanking
you for the interest you have shown in our company.


PARAGRAPH 3

I should be grateful if you would attend our offices for an
interview on @ at @.  Please bring with you documentary
evidence of your age and any examination certificates to
support the qualifications you have listed.


PARAGRAPH 4

Yours sincerely



Marion Winters
Personnel Manager
```

Unit 5: Using stored phrases to create a document

UNIT 4: DEALING WITH PARAGRAPHS

4.3 Moving text in a multipage document

You have no doubt learnt how to move paragraphs or blocks of text before, using the 'Move' or 'Cut and Paste' facility on your word processor. Make sure your instructions are correct, key them into your Checklist, and print out a copy for future reference.

In the following tasks you will not only have to move blocks of text, but you will have to move them to a different page of the document. Some word processing systems have a 'Go To Page . . .' facility, which allows you to key in the number of the page you require and then produces this on the screen. This is very time-saving and means that you do not have to scroll the cursor all the way through the document until you reach the page you want. See if your word processor offers this facility, make a note of how to use it, and when you are sure your instructions are correct, key them into a Checklist.

It is important to remember, when you move text, that it must have a clear line space above and below it if it forms a new paragraph. If the text merely runs on from a previous sentence, the full stop at the end of that sentence must be followed by two clear spaces before the new text begins.

TASK 29

Recall Task 25 and make alterations as shown. Number the second and any subsequent pages. When you have finished, proof read it carefully, then print out one copy.

TASK ~~25~~ **29**

FIRST IMPRESSIONS COUNT

⌈Many firms do not pay sufficient attention to receiving visitors. Customers, clients and callers soon get irritated if their arrival goes unnoticed, or if the receptionist continues chatting and pays no attention to them. It is, therefore, most important to have a receptionist who is alert and aware of her responsibilities and deals with visitors efficiently.⌋

(Move to Ⓐ)

It ~~However, it~~ is not just the receptionist who can create a favourable impression of the firm. If the reception area itself is not clean, tidy and well designed, the visitor can get the wrong idea. Everyone is quick to notice overflowing ashtrays, drooping pot plants or magazines and newspapers which are torn and dog-eared. A general air of neglect makes the visitor think that the firm is not prospering.

✱ **(Insert paragraph here)**
<u>Furniture</u>

Comfortable seating must be installed in the reception area, a coffee table ~~for setting down refreshments,~~ and a coat rack. It is as well to make provision for wet weather by also providing an umbrella stand with a drip pan.

Continued ▶

TASK 35

Using the standard paragraphs stored on disc in Task 34, send a memo to each of the representatives listed in Task 35. Use the paragraphs and infill data indicated. When you have finished, proof read the memos carefully and print out.

TASK 35

1) Paragraph 1   Infill: To John Simpson
                        Ref LS/your initials
                        Today's date

   Paragraph 2   Infill: Northwest regional
                        Adelphi Hotel, Liverpool

   Paragraphs 3 and 6

2) Paragraph 1   Infill: To Martin Jones
                        Ref LS/your initials
                        Today's date

   Paragraph 2   Infill: Midland regional
                        Queens Moat House, Norwich

   Paragraphs 3 and 6

3) Paragraph 1   Infill: To Christine Cookson
                        Ref LS/your initials
                        Today's date

   Paragraph 4   Infill: next Friday

   Paragraphs 5 and 6

▶ *Continued*

Nothing looks so bad as a reception area with dilapidated furniture and a stained carpet, so care must be taken to provide durable seating and stain-resistant flooring.

[### Decor

What is most important is the creation of a warm, pleasant atmosphere with sufficient light for reading. Callers do not want to feel that their visit will be a harrowing experience. This is the effect poor decor can produce.] *(move to ✱)*

Indoor Plants and Flower Arrangements

A visually pleasing environment can be created by the use of pot plants and flowers. They add natural colour to the decor and ~~their flowing lines~~ soften the angular shape of the office fittings.

Newspapers and Magazines

All organisations like to show they are aware of world events, so it is common practice to subscribe to quality newspapers for visitors to read. In addition, many firms provide trade journals in the reception area, together with copies of the latest company newsletter and a display of their most recent products. ~~Obviously, when these become out-of-date, they must be discarded and replaced.~~

Refreshments

It usual to provide the visitor with a hot drink ~~on arrival~~, especially if some delay has occurred or is anticipated before the start of the meeting. Office reception areas are usually equipped with tea and coffee making equipment or provide a vending machine to set the visitor at ease.

△ *(insert paragraph here)*

Key in as the final paragraph:

A good receptionist should have the following qualities in order to prove an asset to the firm:

1) a resourceful nature to cope with all eventualities
2) tactfulness and patience for dealing with difficult callers
3) good office skills and telephonist skills, together with a pleasant speaking voice.

TASK 34

Key in the paragraphs in Task 34 and store for later use. Insert a symbol, as shown, at points where specific information will have to be inserted. Be sure you make a note of the reference under which you have stored each paragraph, as they will be required in Task 35.

TASK 34

PARAGRAPH 1

M E M O R A N D U M

FROM   Linda Scott, Marketing Manager   REF   LS/@

TO   @   DATE @

PARAGRAPH 2

I would like you to attend the @ training course which will be held at the @ on Monday week.

PARAGRAPH 3

The purpose of the course is to impart information about the Japanese way of doing business to representatives who will be launching the communications equipment sales drive in Tokyo.

PARAGRAPH 4

You are requested to attend Head Office for a special training course on Japanese business customs which will be held @.

PARAGRAPH 5

The purpose of the course is to train you as a negotiator to discuss the terms for the launch of an Anglo-Japanese communications satellite in the coming months.

PARAGRAPH 6

I look forward to meeting you on the course and hope that you will find it both informative and enjoyable.

TASK 30

Recall Task 26 and make alterations as shown. Number the second and any subsequent pages. When you have finished, proof read it carefully, then print out one copy.

TASK ~~26~~ 30

~~VISITORS TO THE OFFICE~~

Companies often have strict rules about receiving visitors, in order to prevent industrial espionage and theft, and to ensure that strangers do not wander around the building unattended.

Visitors are usually asked to sign the Visitors' Book or Reception Register on arrival, and may then be given some form of identification, such as a badge or pass. Secretaries are usually telephoned from the reception area so that the visitor can be escorted to the manager's office, provided a prior appointment has been made. (move to ✱)

The Appointments Diary

Visitors can seldom be received without an appointment, but not all managers are willing to devote large periods of time to talking to salesmen or representatives. Often they prefer to restrict the amount of time given to each visitor. It is prudent to discuss with each manager the preferred practice. Common sense also plays a part in making a sensible system, and here are some points to bear in mind.

△ (insert paragraph and adjust the numbering)

1   Before making an appointment, make sure that there are no other events that day or week which would mean that the manager is unable to devote sufficient time to it.

2   Do not make appointments too close to lunchtimes or in the late afternoons in case they run over. This can be most inconvenient.

3   Keep appointments reasonably short so that they do not seem excessively time-consuming if they take longer.

~~4   Never book a manager with appointments all day long. He or she has other commitments each day, and cannot spend the whole time talking to visitors.~~

5   Before the appointment takes place, give the manager the relevant documents to peruse so that he or she knows what the meeting will be about.

6   Note down clearly in the appointments register the visitor's name, designation and organisation with a brief statement giving the reason for the visit, so that there is no misunderstanding when the visitor arrives.

Continued ▶

UNIT 5

INSERTING STORED TEXT
5.2
Using stored phrases to create a document

The phrases that you stored in Task 32 can be accessed to create complete documents. Obviously, the choice of phrases and paragraphs picked will make the documents created differ from one another.

Using your WP manual make notes on how to access stored phrases and paragraphs. It may be that you have to create a new blank document first, but this may not be the case. Test your notes on Task 33 and if they are correct key them into a Checklist and print out a copy.

TASK 33

Using the standard paragraphs stored on disc in Task 32, send a letter to each of the firms listed in Task 33, who have enquired about communications products. Use today's date and the reference FR/your initials. When you have finished, proof read the letters carefully and print out.

TASK 33

1) Benson Telecommunications Ltd
   Merefield Industrial Park
   NORTHAMPTON   NN3 3GE

   Paragraphs 1, 3 and 5.

2) Jupiter Business Machines Ltd
   16 Central Highway
   MILTON KEYNES   MK2 7LJ

   Paragraphs 1, 2 and 5.

3) Bagshot Electronics Ltd
   16 Peacock Parade
   PORTSMOUTH   HA2 1YD
   For the attention of Mr H Jackson

   Paragraphs 1, 4 and 5.

▶ Continued

7. Be prepared to rescue a manager from appointments which are ~~clearly~~ overrunning by providing a plausible excuse. Sometimes, of course, it is clear that the appointment is intended to continue.

8. Make sure that the visitor is offered (tea or coffee) either before or during the appointment, in accordance with the firm's established practice.

9. If there is too much pressure for appointments, enquire whether other members of the department can receive visitors. Very often, section heads will relieve the pressure by receiving some of the ~~firm's visitors~~ callers.

10. When a caller arrives without an appointment, do not confirm that the manager is in the office without first finding out if he or she wants to see the visitor or not. [move to △]

※ (insert paragraph here)

Useful Information Sources

The receptionist would be well advised to keep some helpful information sources to hand. An essential item is the current version of the company's internal telephone directory giving the names, designations, locations and extension numbers of the firm's personnel. A telephone message pad or notebook for taking down messages and making a log of visitors to the firm is also indispensable.

Other useful items are a set of telephone and fax directories, a streetfinder and British Rail timetables. Duplicate maps of the firm's premises and the locality would also be helpful to guide visitors.

For emergencies, it would also be wise to have a list of managers' and security officers' home telephone numbers, the company doctor or nurse and a first aid kit and illustrated manual.

> Key this in as paragraph 10.
>
> As visitors leave, you may have to ask them to sign out. Even if this is not the case, you should note each departure by saying something like 'Thank you for calling, goodbye'.

▶ Continued

PARAGRAPH 3

We enclose the specification and technical details of the particular model you require, and confirm that you would be entitled to a trade discount of 33 per cent. However, we would urge you to make an appointment with one of our technical staff to provide an on-site assessment of your requirements. This service is entirely free, and in most parts of the country can be provided on the next working day.

PARAGRAPH 4

We have passed on your details to our local area representative, who will be contacting you within two days. A demonstration can then be arranged at a mutually convenient time. In the meantime, we enclose our Corporate Information Pack for your perusal. It gives full details of the latest computer communications technology developed by our company and explains our philosophy of supplying leading computer products to the business community at a price that is the envy of our rivals, and with no compromises on quality, delivery, service or support.

PARAGRAPH 5

Our equipment has an excellent reputation for reliability and comes with a one-year guarantee and maintenance contract. However, should there be any problem during this period, our engineers are on 24-hour call out. Should you decide to make a purchase, you will also receive our money-back undertaking. This means that if you are not entirely satisfied with our hardware product, or if you merely wish to change your mind, you may return it within thirty days for a full refund.

Yours faithfully

FRANCES ROBINSON
Marketing Manager

Enc

TASK 31

This is a timed task which should take you no longer than 40 minutes to complete and print out.

Recall Task 27 and break it into three pages, making alterations as shown. Number the second and third pages. When you have finished, proof read it carefully and print out one copy.

TASK ~~27~~ **31**

            M E M O R A N D U M

TO   All WP Secretaries   REF   JS/MC

FROM   Office Services Manager   DATE   (Insert today's date)

The computer section have now ~~produced~~ **completed** their ~~report on~~ **study of** the use of electronic 'information managers', which we are hoping to install in the New Year. For those of you who are not acquainted with this term, an 'information manager' is a software package which provides a computer-based diary, address book and notepad. Apart from making and viewing entries, it enables you to make lists, calculate expenses, write letters and manage your time more efficiently.

(Insert paragraph A here)

I am giving a brief explanation ~~below~~ on the use of the diary and address book facilities, and will be arranging a demonstration and question-and-answer session in the near future.

Training sessions will, of course, take place as soon as the software is purchased. **It is not envisaged that this will happen for at least several weeks.**

WHAT **EXACTLY** IS AN ELECTRONIC DIARY? An electronic diary is a software package which replaces the traditional book-bound method of regulating the way diaries and appointments are kept. The packages available are integrated and link various familiar features.

These features are all subject to the use of a security password agreed within the organisation.

    1   word processing and electronic notepad
    2   spreadsheet and database
    3   communications
    4   calculator ~~and~~ **five-year calendar reference tables**
    5

Inset by 13mm (½")

Paragraph A
Many brands of software are now on the market and they have all been tested extensively on our equipment.

Continued ▶

Unit 4: Moving text in a multipage document

INSERTING STORED TEXT

5·1 Storing phrases

This unit gives you more practice on moving text around. To minimise the amount of keying in you have to do, word processors have the ability to merge stored phrases or paragraphs into a new document (or set of documents). Sometimes, the term 'boilerplating' is used to describe this use of standard phrases and paragraphs.

Before word processors came into use, standard phrases or paragraphs had to be typed separately each time a new document was required. This meant that they were typed over and over again. Nowadays, it is possible to use the word processor to store a whole bank of commonly used phrases or paragraphs and just recall them when they are required.

First study your word processor manual and make brief notes on how to store phrases and paragraphs. Some systems use a 'Library Document Facility' for this. Others require you to key the work into separate files. Then test out your notes on the first task. If they are correct, key them into a Checklist for future reference.

TASK 32

Key in the paragraphs in Task 32 and store for later use. Be sure you make a note of the reference under which you have stored each one, as they will be required in Task 33.

```
TASK 32

PARAGRAPH 1

Dear Sir/Madam

Thank you for your recent letter which expressed an interest
in our new range of computer communications equipment.  With
our experienced engineering and design team, some of the most
modern production facilities available in Europe, and annual
sales in excess of £200 million, we are now the largest
computer communications manufacturer in the world.


PARAGRAPH 2

We enclose a full colour brochure and current price list, our
most comprehensive to date.  The specifications and technical
details of each model are listed in the brochure, together
with a general description, and we are confident that you will
find an item to suit your requirements.  We would call your
attention to our wide product range backed by unrivalled
service and support, and our outstanding deals on network
hardware.
```

▶ Continued

▶ Continued

FEATURES OF THE ELECTRONIC DIARY These features are all subject to the use of a security password agreed within the organisation.

(insert paragraph B here)

1. The actual diary and appointments facility allows a five-year calendar and rolling diary to be scanned. Entries can be made using the ~~word~~ text processing facility.

2. Diary pages can be viewed either quickly or slowly, and the day is divided into morning, afternoon and evening. It is also possible to view by week, month or year.

3. Appointments and reminders can be entered at any time or place and for any duration. Periods can be 'booked' or removed to indicate that no interruption should be made to work. Reminders can be inserted and jobs for the day can be prioritised - even well in advance of the day concerned! A link with the electronic notepad can allow more lengthy messages to be accessed to serve as memory joggers.

4. Networking ~~A link with a local area network~~ means that the diaries of personnel within the building can be searched, and arrangements made and entered for meetings at a mutually convenient time and date. It is also possible to order transport, equipment or accommodation from a central office services area.

5. Other packages can also be used and incorporated in the diary. Word processing is the most commonly used of these packages.

Training sessions will, of course, take place as soon as the software is purchased.

Paragraph B

There are numerous advantages in using an electronic diary. Meetings can be arranged for several managers simultaneously on a mutually convenient date. This can be done without running around from office to office to see when managers are free. However, the main features of the electronic diary are as follows:

Continued ▶

▶ Continued

THE ADDRESS BOOK The address book is arranged in alphabetical order and will ~~probably~~ be displayed on screen like open pages of a traditional address book. After selecting the correct letter of the alphabet, you can then key in a person's name, company address, phone and fax numbers.

(Insert paragraph C here)

You will be able to use the address book to do other tasks, such as making lists of all the people connected with a particular firm, or all the firms selling a certain product. This is done by using the database facility and making a mini database for each category you want to list.

The electronic notepad is useful here, as you can key in additional information about the categories you have created. You can also set up letter templates and automatically insert details, such as name, address and date, from either the address book or the database.

You can even keep track of expenses, such as telephone calls or faxes, by using the integrated calculator. This can be done for individuals or categories.

Paragraph C

Details can be copied from one person's address book to another, and secretaries and managers can all look at the same address book, if necessary. Entries can be made or deleted with the greatest of ease, and print-outs of an alphabetical section made when required. Not only is the electronic address book simple to use, but it is also very time-saving.